"God's Got This..."

the 3 little words every woman wants to hear

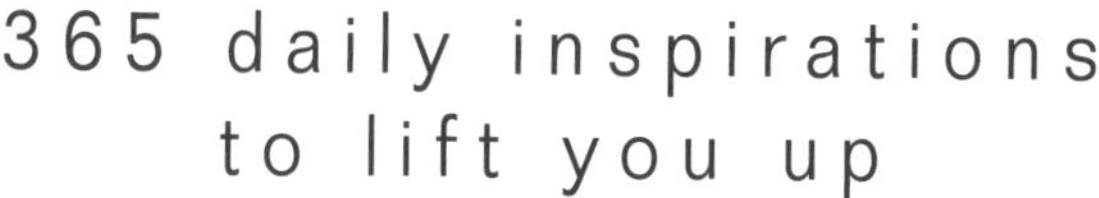

"God's Got This..."

ISBN 978-0-9987685-1-9

Published by Product Concept Mfg., Inc.
2175 N. Academy Circle #200, Colorado Springs, CO 80909

Written and Compiled by Patricia Mitchell in association with Product Concept, Inc.

All scripture quotations are from the King James version of the Bible unless otherwise noted.

Start your morning on a positive note with Three Little Words. With a snippet of lighthearted wisdom for each day of the year, this book reminds you that the hours ahead of you offer a unique opportunity to smile, laugh, play, hope, love, celebrate, and give thanks. It's just another way to say the Three Little Words every woman wants (and needs!) to hear...
GOD'S GOT THIS!

1

See the Possibilities

We can get so used to things as they've always been that we think, "This is the way they have to stay." Maybe so...but maybe not. Perhaps there are choices and changes available to you that would make your life better, easier, and maybe even pack a few more smiles. Look outside the boundaries of "the way it's always been" and see the possibilities!

2

For Instant Impressions

There are people around you who do and say beautiful things. Examples? Think of the family member who encourages you, the friend with a great sense of humor, the coworker who knows how to make the best of every situation, the retail associate who always has a smile on her face. If you want to add beauty to the world (and be beautiful, too), copy them!

3 *Beyond First Impressions*

First impressions are all about appearance. That's all–they can't see the real person hiding behind the eye-catching clothes or the gentle spirit sheltering inside a rough exterior. When you meet people for the first time, you'll get a first impression of who they might be. But give yourself time to discover who they really are.

4 *Room for Improvement*

Few of us are in top-notch physical condition or at complete peace with ourselves and with others. How about you? Name one thing that you'd like to raise a notch or two and create a plan of action. Small, practical steps that you can take each day will get you further than a grand resolution! A written reminder helps to keep you going.

5

Circle of Friends

Friends who have known you for decades have shared many of your childhood experiences. New friends know you as the person you are today, and they're partners with you in the joys and challenges you have right now. Do more than send a text to keep in touch with all your friends. Call frequently, or better yet, get together face-to-face!

6

Clear the Clutter

Dishes in the sink, last night's snack bag open on the couch, clothes hanging off chairs, and unmade beds are hardly a welcoming sight! Spend a few minutes every day clearing the clutter before you leave for work. When you get home, you'll step into a pleasant, organized space. And even better, you'll be able to find the remote control!

7 *Call to Attention*

The day is filled with so many little, repetitive tasks—paying bills, buying groceries, parking the car, answering the phone, grabbing a bite for lunch. Do them mindfully. Add an elegant swoosh when you sign your name. Use a friendly tone of voice when you speak. Chew slowly and attentively. You'll enrich your day. You'll enrich your life.

8 *Speak with Authority*

Kind words and polite behavior are compatible with direct speech. Listen to yourself. Do your requests sound tentative? Do statements come across as questions begging for judgment? Do you back down at the slightest hint of disapproval? If you respect the views and opinions of others, respect your own. Speak kindly, politely, and authoritatively.

9 *Today and Tomorrow*

This moment is the one you have right now—make the most of it! But keep an eye on the future, too. Cultivate your thoughts concerning what you would like your life to look like, say, five or ten years from now. Where would you live? What would you be doing? Goals for tomorrow add meaning and purpose to what you're doing today!

10 *Your First Love*

Remember what you loved as a kid? Like music, sports, technology, dance, film, art, writing–you name it. Perhaps your career or responsibilities make it impossible to pursue your first love fulltime, but don't let it linger in the past. Find a way to play around with it. As an enriching and enjoyable hobby, your first love will bring back the child in you!

11 *Choose Good People*

You can't always avoid difficult people, but you can minimize their effect on your mood and self-confidence. Outweigh their negative words with a positive response, even if you have to grit your teeth to do so. Balance their impact on you by listening to and surrounding yourself with people who uplift, encourage, and value you.

12 *Your Spa Day*

A day at the spa–ahhh! You relax in comfort while expert hands massage neck and back, muscles and joints. Frustrations slip away, and you leave renewed and revitalized. It's similar to what happens when you spend time reflecting on God's love for you and His presence in your life. His spa for your soul is free, and it's one you can visit any time you like. Like now.

13 *Laugh Right Now*

Remember the time you were lost and drove around an hour before you stopped and asked directions? When the kids volunteered you as chaperone for their overnight camp out? At the moment, it wasn't funny, but you can laugh about it now. So why not take a shortcut and laugh when it happens? Laughter doesn't take away frustrations, but it sure makes them easier to take!

14 *Good for You*

Get a funny joke or inspirational quote delivered to your inbox each day. Look out the window and really focus on one thing you see every morning. Make it a goal to greet a stranger or ask a coworker how she's doing. Decide to be happy. Choose to keep going. Every day, do something good for yourself.

15

Step Up Anyway

It's easier to cancel the doctor's appointment than to keep it. More comfortable not to say anything than to tackle a sticky situation. Safer to bail out than to take on the project and risk failure. Simpler to decide it's hopeless than to do what you can to make it better. When you feel you're not up to it, step up anyway. Be brave!

16

Creatures of Habit

Today's habits are tomorrow's reality. Are your current eating and exercising habits conducive to later health and well-being? Are your present-day thoughts, words, and actions pointing to future emotional and financial stability? Are the skills you're developing in this season of life likely to enhance the next? If not, now is the time to make some changes!

17 *Be a Dabbler*

Just because you were interested in something at one time doesn't mean you have to keep at it forever. Same with the sassy look you adopted years ago and are still sporting. The menu choices that haven't changed for decades. Quitting isn't always bad. Try things you've never done before. Dabble around until you come up with things that express the woman you are today!

18 *Relationship How-To*

Navigating relationships isn't easy. Besides, there are so many of them—family, friends, workplace, clubs, church, community! Navigation success includes treating all your relationships with appropriate speech and behavior; showing consideration for the feelings, fears, and burdens of each person; being there for them whenever you're needed. Enhance their lives, and they will enhance yours.

19 *Stay in Control*

There's a difference between a passion and an obsession. A passion for doing your best engages you with life, but an obsession with perfectionism drains your energy. A passion for sports or painting or technology enlivens you, but an obsession with any one thing encloses you in a very small world. If it's a passion, you control it. If it's an obsession, it controls you.

20 *A Smile Today*

Even if you're in a less-than-happy place right now, there's something good in it. How you're carrying your burden might be showing someone else how to better carry theirs. Your current challenge is building empathy for others who may face a similar circumstance later on. Go deep within yourself, and you might find that there's a smile, even in a struggle!

21 *It's About You*

To think well of others, you have to think well of yourself. Name your talents and celebrate the joy of them, if only to the face you see in the mirror. Say something uplifting to yourself every day–a friendly word will do. Be glad to be you, warts and all. Only those who possess a sense of self-worth can truly appreciate the worth of someone else.

22 *Smile of Gratitude*

"If you can't be thankful for what you have, be thankful for what you don't have!" That's one way of looking at it, but the best way is still the old-fashioned way. Count your blessings, because they really count. Appreciate the beautiful, heartening, joyful, fun, and fantastic things in life, because they're really there. Practice gratitude–it's what really happy people do.

23 *There for You*

When you choose your friends, choose friends you can trust. Those who speak well of you even when they're around people you're unlikely to ever meet. Those you can depend on to care about you as a person, and not just for what you can do for them or the role you fill in their lives. Pick friends who have your back, just as you have theirs. Those are true friends!

24 *Check the Results*

If you want to know what's working, check the results. Repeated disappointment might indicate a need for knowledgeable guidance or helpful advice. Continual frustration could mean that a time of rest and reassessment is in order. Numerous confrontations may suggest that there are better ways of asserting yourself. Check how things are going by checking the results.

25 *Lessen the Stress*

A little stress is good. It's invigorating and motivating. Nothing but stress, however, is not so good. Day after day tension keeps you on edge, drains your energy, and undermines physical and emotional well-being. If a good night's sleep doesn't take care of a day's stress, be proactive. Make necessary changes before stress drives you to your wits' end!

26

Happy If Only

"I'd be happy if only..." Those are dangerous words! You would be happy if only a certain person or situation would change...if only you had made a different choice...if only you could buy this or that. Beware! Remind yourself of this truth: Happiness comes from inside. When you have it, outside reality doesn't change it. When you don't have it, outside reality won't change it.

27

Like Attracts Like

If you want to attract positive, enthusiastic, interesting people, it's not hard. Just be that kind of person yourself! As the saying goes, "Birds of a feather flock together." Radiate warmth with your smile. Highlight your talents by getting involved with others. Talk about what's right with the world. It won't take long before you're a welcome member of the best kind of flock!

28

A Good Lesson

It's unmistakable about mistakes–they teach you what not to do next time! Lick your wounds, but give a nod of thanks for the lesson learned or the refresher course obviously needed. Think through how you're going to handle yourself next time and the decisions you will make when similar circumstances arise. In short, never let a good mistake go to waste!

29

Way of Speaking

On social media, you come across a post so poorly written that you simply scroll right on by. On TV, you listen to uncivil ranting for only a few minutes before changing the channel. No matter who or where you are, what you say may be worthwhile, but the way you say it determines whether anyone sticks around to listen.

30 *A Grace-full Idea*

There's something uniquely grace-full about saying grace before meals. A few words of prayer season the food with the spice of gratitude, the sweetness of goodwill, the tang of contentment. Whether your next meal is a five-course dinner or a bologna sandwich, do something graceful. A short prayer is a gracious, soul-lifting interlude of looking up before digging in!

31 *This Is Contentment*

Uplift your spirit and enrich your life by changing the scenery. No, you don't have to buy new furniture or book a trip to some exotic destination. Rather, shift the focus of your thoughts and attention away from what you want to what you have. What you want might become reality, or it might not. Either way, it's in the future. What you have is right now. Enjoy the scenery!

FEBRUARY

1 *The Best Light*

Have you ever noticed how magical faces look by candlelight? Flickering shadows hide flaws and make expressions look mysterious and appealing. The same can be said when you speak well of others and of yourself. Put others, including yourself, in the best light by relating words and actions in the kindest possible way and in harmony with the truth.

2 *It's Good Exercise!*

There are lots of ways to get exercise besides exercising! Park in a spot farthest from your workplace or grocery store and walk to the door. When there's a call for table-and-chairs set-up for a meeting, answer it. When there's a choice between taking a bus or hoofing it, hoof it. If there are stairs, take them. You'd be surprised how much exercise you can squeeze in a day!

3 *Line of Sight*

What you see is what you get–well, sometimes. When it comes to spiritual matters, you can't see God's great love, but you have it. You can't see His presence, but it's there. You can't see His good plans for your life, but they will unfold in time. Remember that there's more–much more!–around you and ahead of you than you can see!

4

Have a Plan

When you have a plan for tomorrow, you'll wake up in the morning with a feeling of control and expectation. You know what you need to do, your appointments don't come as a last-minute surprise, and you've made choices about what you will do in your free time. Plan your work, and you'll be excited to work your plan!

5

Savor Your Stage

Each life stage opens different opportunities. Kids, for example, are at the optimum ages for soaking up knowledge that will prepare them for the future. Midlife is a perfect time to grow in experience, involvement, character, and wisdom. Older years bring the blessings of increased insight, perception, and understanding. Wherever you are in life, savor it to the fullest!

6

Onto Plan B

You may have had the perfect plans. They were vetted by parents and teachers. You did everything you were supposed to do–then what did you get? The absolute opposite of what you deserved! Your disappointment is heartbreaking, but don't let it keep you down. There's always a Plan B–and sometimes, it turns out better than you could have imagined!

7 *The Grand Design*

Busy with day-to-day activities, you might lose track of your place in God's overall design. Take some time out today to reflect on how your current reality reflects God's care for you and His love for others. Note the things you are doing to act as His heart and hands in the world. In God's grand design, there you are!

8 *Picture Your Purpose*

Say you're working at something that isn't really your dream job. So ask yourself why you're doing it. Is it to save money for a house? Make the rent or mortgage? Pay off student loans? Take a nice vacation next year? Whatever your purpose, put a picture of it in front of you to remind you of why you're doing what you're doing!

9 *Control Your Time*

They say that if you want something done, ask a busy person! And if you're someone others always call on, you need to know how to say "no." The word might not flow easily from your lips, but for your health and sanity, you cannot cram into your day every to-do that others might want to give you. Take control of your time–it's yours, after all!

10 *Ahead of You*

Wherever you would like to go in life, others have gone before you. Find out what they have done to succeed. If possible, sit down with them and ask them to share their thoughts and experience. Most people will be honored to have the privilege of helping another person advance. You'll certainly gain knowledge, and maybe a willing mentor, too!

11 *Listen to Success*

Naysayers are all too eager to point out all the disadvantages you face and all the hindrances standing in the way of your success. Perhaps they feel that they couldn't make it, given your situation. Instead, listen to people whose own achievements motivate them to offer real and practical help and advice. Listen to those who say, "You can make it, too!"

12 *It's Your Day!*

Every so often, plan a play day. All day long, do what relaxes and rejuvenates you, body and spirit. Maybe you'll go home, pull the shades, shut off the phone, and lie on the couch binge-watching your favorite movies. Or you'll call as many friends as you can muster to join you for a potluck picnic. Your choice! Whatever it is, enjoy!

13 *Enough is Enough*

Pizza is a tasty treat, but after the third, fourth, and fifth slices, it might not taste so good anymore. Possessions add convenience, comfort, and delight to life, but an overload brings on a lot of maintenance tasks, not to mention debt. The key to contentment is knowing when enough is just that–enough.

14 *Tag the Time*

Holidays, anniversaries, birthdays, graduations–each one marks a particular time in the year or milestone in your life. Why let Christmas come and go without taking time out to celebrate its true meaning? Why let your special days get buried under the appointments and have-to's of an ordinary day? Tag the time. Make memories. Celebrate seriously!

15 *In Your Skin*

Have you ever passed a store window and seen your reflection as you walk by? If you noticed anything short of erect posture, confident strides, and comfortable-in-my-skin appearance, it's time to make some changes. Practice positive body language. It helps you feel good about yourself, promotes good health, and, when you're in public, contributes to your safety.

16 *Feelings Are Fleeting*

Most of us, at some point in life, have become so enthusiastic that we impulsively say "yes." It might be a major purchase–but after seeing our credit card bill, we regret having bought it. Or a promise to a person–but when passion cools, we realize we have made a mistake. Give your emotions two good companions: reason and judgment.

17 *What Comes First?*

Life that is first about self is a very limited one as it chases passing whims and selfish goals. It pursues its own pleasures, but finds nothing satisfying. Life that is first about others has no boundaries. Opportunities to do, serve, and love keep on growing! Though too busy to look for it, the life that puts others first finds lasting joy!

18 *Do the Footwork*

You can't solve every problem, but you can take practical steps toward making it less of a problem. Though others may not be open to change, you can change your response to them. Not every element of an issue lies under your control, but you can use what influence you have for the better. Then, let it be. You have done everything you can do.

19 *Contentment Is Peace*

Compare yourself to others, and the door to discontentment swings wide open. Shut it immediately! Center your heart and mind on everything precious to you–the people you love, the memories you cherish, the hopes you have for the future. Don't give away your peace of mind. And whenever you start thinking that your neighbor's grass is greener, just imagine what his water bill must look like!

20 *Three for Faith*

Though faith itself is a gift from God, there are three things you can do to nourish and strengthen it: Daily Bible reading, time out for prayer and reflection, and deliberate application of God's guidelines to your everyday words and actions. In time, these things will become second-nature to you, as well as observable and objective evidence of God's presence in your life.

21 *There's Enough Time*

Why waste the small spaces of a day? Ten minutes spent waiting for a friend, a quarter-hour before you need to leave the house, an interval between appointments. Use them! If you're at home, straighten a room or rinse the dishes. When you're out, notice your surroundings and pick out something interesting. Put a book on a device you carry with you so you can read anywhere.

22 *Expect the Good*

You never know what a day will bring! An email from the manager telling you you're hired...or promoted. A text from a friend to ask if you can go with her on a dream vacation. A phone call from a loved one who can't wait to share her good news. Greet each day with a sense of expectancy!

23 *All of Us*

If you work with a group in any setting, you're surrounded by people with different talents and strengths. As long as everyone keeps their eyes on a common goal, each person's contribution helps to make it happen. Use your influence, whether as leader or team member, to make sure everyone receives recognition and appreciation for their efforts.

24

Support the Truth

Never underestimate the power of media to sway your opinion to their way of thinking, or to persuade you that their video depicts exactly what happened. If their views have validity and their pictures reflect reality, they will hold up to checking, cross-checking, and double-checking. Suspend belief until you know what you're believing.

25

Toward Sweet Dreams

Few meaningful and worthwhile hopes and dreams come true in an instant. Usually it takes years of daily effort before a vision for the future begins to take the shape of reality. A few setbacks? They're bound to happen! And when you work through them, your dream-come-true will be all the sweeter for you!

26

Way to Happiness

Focus on your spiritual growth and intellectual development. Take on your responsibilities with wholehearted acceptance and make choices that support the well-being of those around you. It's not the way that reason would tell you leads to happiness, but it's the way that happiness opens you to receive it.

27

Practice Makes Perfect

Perhaps you have a few things that you plan to change...someday. Say, getting more sleep. Eating better. Exercising more. Spending less. Making a budget. Getting organized. But why wait? Commit yourself to one–only one!–item and start putting it into practice right now. Keep it up every day, and soon it won't come as a struggle, but as second-nature to you!

28

For the Good

What do you like most about yourself? Don't be shy–name it! Perhaps it's your bubbly personality, your attractive appearance, your high IQ, your achievements so far, your talents and abilities. Yet remember that whatever you named is God's gift to you, not a cause for pride or conceit. Whatever you like most about yourself, use it for the good of all.

1 *That's Some Body!*

Have you ever told your feet, knees, and hips how glad you are for all they do? Or your fingers how much you appreciate their help in opening a jar... picking up a shoe...holding a child's hand? Your heart for pumping, your lungs for breathing, your brain for thinking? Your body does marvelous things! Next time you're soaping it down in the shower, give it a round of applause!

2 *Tour the Town*

Have you ever played tourist right where you live and work? Visited its museums and galleries, read up on its history...sampled different restaurants, taken photos of places that catch your eye? Discover the noteworthy people who have lived there...the significant events that have taken place... the fascinating facts you've never heard before. Play the tourist this weekend!

3 *Never Give Up!*

It's unfortunate if you would decide to give up on a worthwhile goal, but heartbreaking if you should give up on yourself. No matter how many steps back you have gone, there's always a step forward... and another...and another. Promise yourself that you'll never give up on yourself, because God never, ever will!

4 *It's a Priority*

Your priorities are important, but just as important are the priorities of others. Build new relationships and strengthen old ones by listening and understanding the priorities of those around you. When a conflict arises between your vision and theirs, sit down together and hash out a consensus. That way, you won't be butting heads, but heading in the same direction.

5 *"Good" Won't Do!*

How are you doing? "Good" won't make it as an answer this time! Take a few moments to objectively assess where you are in personal health and fitness, spiritual maturity, relationships with others, financial stability, workplace or community standing, and overall satisfaction. Specify an area that needs the most improvement and plan a practical course of action.

6 *Primed for Adventure*

An adventurous life looks like this: You are willing to take risks after weighing the pros and cons. You say "yes" instead of "no" when there's an opportunity to challenge yourself or try something that just might scare you a little. You approach each new life stage as an opening rather than a closing. You are well-primed for adventure, so live adventurously!

7 *A Curious Thing*

If you're curious about an event, explore it. Find relevant background material online, or at a library or museum. Talk to eyewitnesses, if any, or historians. Take on the role of a responsible journalist and record the facts as you learn them, including conflicting viewpoints. For sure you'll have something interesting to talk about at your next get-together with friends–and maybe get a spot in your local newspaper!

8 *A Healthy Head*

Just as it's vital to take care of your physical health, it's just as necessary to tend to your mental health. Keep your emotional boundaries in good repair. Ask for time-out when your nerves are frazzled. Talk to a trusted friend, therapist, or minister if your thoughts are becoming frequently muddled or confused, or if your actions are causing others to ask if you're okay. Take care of you.

9 *Make It Personal*

Personalize your space. If you create art, hang or display a few of the pieces you like. If you've traveled, frame photos or set out souvenirs that remind you of a marvelous trip. On your phone and computer, choose a picture of your loved ones or a favorite place for your wallpaper. Let the little things around you bring a smile to your face!

10 *In the Game*

It's no secret that technology changes quickly. Keep up by learning what new devices can do, and use those that prove useful to you. If you're in the workplace, you'll be ahead of the game if you're known as someone who eagerly and comfortably adapts to change. But whatever your age or stage in life, you don't want to become a stranger in an increasingly technology-centered world.

11 *Feel the Beat*

Be attentive to how the music you hear affects how you feel. Does it energize you, or put your teeth on edge? Does it relax you, or bore you? Does it convey an uplifting mood, or an angry, violent one? For your personal listening pleasure, choose your music as you would choose your feelings.

12 *You're the Story*

Several online sites provide a place for you to post favorite pictures, projects, ideas, and sayings. Try looking at your cyber collection with the eyes of a casual visitor. What colors predominate? What life views are represented? What images show up repeatedly, though in various forms? It's just another way of getting to know yourself and what you really, really like!

13 *Just Hang On!*

When daily stress and frustrations take you to the end of your rope...tie a knot and hang on! Hang on to confidence in your ability to get through this tough time, just as you have all the tough times behind you. Hang on to the encouragement you've heard and the praise you've received. Most of all, hang on to God. Hang on, because He will see you through.

14 *Care for Yourself*

If you sit down most of the day, stand up. Find something that gets you moving, like walking or bicycling, swimming or dancing. But if you're on your feet most of the day, sit down. Do something that relaxes your mind as well as your body–read, listen to music, or just doze off for a little bit. Whatever you do, take care of yourself!

15 *Play It Right*

Other people are not necessarily going to act according to your playbook. Given this inescapable reality, watch how many pet peeves and social irritations you write into your script. It can become so clogged with petty annoyances that everything you utter is suffused with anger! Life is too short for that. Save your fury for worthwhile themes.

16 *Do the Unexpected*

Others depend on you to take care of certain responsibilities and meet particular obligations. Because you do, it means that you're someone who's reliable and likely to come through when you're called on. That's to your credit, but don't let it debit your spontaneity fund. Draw from it occasionally. Give yourself the freedom to step away and just do your own thing once in a while.

17 *No Bad Days*

What are you going to allow to ruin your day? Surely not the way your hair turned out or a chipped fingernail. Or the driver who cut you off in traffic. Or the mean-spirited debate on the radio this morning. So what matters so much to you that you will allow it to ruin your day? Ask yourself that question before you even think about having a bad day!

18 *A Better Card*

You might know someone who plays the misery card. She lives from grievance to grievance, becoming a perpetual sufferer. While it's true that no one can know (or has a right to judge) the depth of your feelings, there comes a time to toss the misery card and play another hand. A happier, more resilient, more forward-moving one!

19 *Show of Values*

You know the messages and images that repulse you, offend you, drag you down, or demean your beliefs and values. When these things are maliciously paraded in front of you, you don't have to stand around and watch. Intolerant? Not at all. You're not saying they cannot be there. You're just saying you cannot be there.

20 *Those Around You*

Among the people you interact with regularly, who are the ones you can go to when something is on your mind? You can trust them to keep your confidence if you ask them to. You know they will hear you out and offer insightful comments and useful advice. These are your go-to people whenever you need help, motivation, and encouragement!

21

You're Looking Good

Today, anything goes when it comes to clothes. Thank goodness you have the freedom to make your own choices! Yet the choices you make display your sense of style and appropriateness. They also reveal whether you think you (and those around you) are worth the trouble it takes to dress smartly. It doesn't take a lot of money–just a few smart choices.

22

A Balanced Life

A balanced diet consists of a variety of foods, not just one–even if that one is kale! And just as the body needs diversity, so do your mind and spirit. Balance work-time with time for rest and relaxation. Play heartily. Laugh freely. Take delight in small luxuries and simple pleasures. You might be surprised how much better you feel when it's time to get back to work again!

23 *Ask for Help*

No one knew she was struggling to keep up. He never told anyone he didn't understand how to go about his task. Yet there were friends and coworkers who would have been happy to offer help and support, if only they had known. What felt like personal failure to her...to him...was only a failure to ask for help. When you need it, ask for it!

24 *Start the Day*

If your mornings are hectic, it's time to revamp your routine. Describe what you'd like your mornings to look, sound, and feel like, and then see how much you can realistically put into practice. Perhaps you'll need to set the alarm a little earlier to allow extra time, but just think how nice it would be to start your day refreshed rather than rushed!

25 *End of Day*

A warm shower...comfortable room temperature... soft, relaxing music...night clothes that feel good against your skin (and look good on you, too!)... cozy covers for the bed...a word of thanks for all the blessings received. That's not a bad way to end the day. Think about your bedtime ritual. Does it lead to sweet dreams? What can you do to make it that way?

26 *The Bigger Picture*

You're part of the big picture. In it, you have a role to play, a role that takes you beyond your personal needs and wants. What might your bigger-than-you role be? Perhaps as a volunteer for a charitable organization, worker or speaker on behalf of a social or political effort, or, along with others, a campaigner for a cause you believe in. Where are you in the bigger picture?

27 *A Wonderful List*

Sometime during the day, quickly and off the top of your head list all the wonderful things about you that you can think of! Don't stop to change or edit your words. And don't worry, no one's looking, and you don't even have to hit "save" on your screen. When you've run out of words, look back over your list. It's sure to make you feel beyond wonderful!

28 *The Real You*

Each year and each season of life brings you more knowledge about yourself. You begin to acknowledge your real thoughts, not those handed down to you. Your real dreams, not those suggested by social norms. Yes, you're coming into your own, becoming your own person. How can you more fully explore and discover the real you?

29 *Up-Front Confidence*

Most of us put up a brave face. We don't want to appear insecure or unsure in front of others, and yet we often feel that way. Actually, the confidence we show on the outside has a way of easing feelings of unworthiness or ineptitude on the inside. But when you need a little extra encouragement, fess up. Your trusted friends will understand completely!

30 *Banish the Boasting*

It's one thing to share your accomplishments with others, but quite another to trumpet them. Sure, others are more than likely to heap compliments and congratulations on you every time you mention your latest success, but wouldn't their words be sweeter if you let them bring up the subject first? Make sure you're giving them the chance!

31 *A Mysterious Subject*

How comfortable are you with mysteries? With things called miracles, and with facts that can't be easily explained away? When it comes to matters of the spirit–like the workings of your own soul–you're entering a mysterious landscape, indeed. Explore, experience, discover what you can. And then rest content in God's loving presence. No other answers needed.

APRIL

1 *They Go Together*

Confidence and humility make good companions. Confidence enables you to tell a good story, relate a funny joke, or talk about what's going on in your life. But suppose someone or something interrupts you. Then humility enables you to wait until your listeners ask you to resume. And if they don't? Well, maybe it was time for the conversation to shift directions anyway!

2 *You Are Forgiven*

It's usually easier to forgive others than to forgive ourselves. Perhaps the words of apology we may hear, or the sympathy of others who know we've been wronged, leads us to forgive. But our own shortcomings are more complex. We're loathe to accept our own apology. That's why God longs to whisper the words our repentant hearts need to hear: "You are forgiven."

3 *Enjoy the Process*

Have you ever looked forward to a vacation with so much excitement that you could hardly think of anything else? While the trip itself was fun and memorable, so was your eager anticipation. Give your present a dash of excitement by planning a trip, adventure, or experience for the future. The fun begins the minute you start thinking about it!

4 *A Better Idea*

As a child, you imagined what life would be like when you grew up. Just for fun, write down some of the things you thought. Perhaps a few projections were accurate, but probably most were not. Of those "nots," how many linger in your mind as how things should be? Give the innocent little girl in you a big hug, and then tell her, "That's not the way it turned out. It's better!"

5 *A Golden Reputation*

A good reputation, built up over years of faithfulness to family, loyalty to community, and selfless living, can end in an instant. All it takes is one ethical shortcut, one lapse in judgment, one underhanded deal. Yes, there is forgiveness, no matter what happened. But a tainted reputation is never completely pure again. Guard your reputation–it's more valuable than gold.

6 *Pray it Forward*

When someone pays you a nice compliment or does a favor for you, thank the person, of course. And then let your heart thank God for their presence in your life. Ask Him to bless them twice over! In the following days, look for a kindness you can do for someone else–and don't be surprised if another blessing makes its way to you!

7 *In their Shoes*

Do you always completely agree with your loved ones? Do you see eye-to-eye with your neighbors, coworkers, and club members every time? Probably not! Rather than refute their opinion, however, find out more about it. Try to put yourself in their shoes and understand why they feel the way they do. Treat them as reasonable, intelligent human beings–same as you are!

8 *World of Wonders*

Do some traveling via cyberspace! Pick a country and learn the basics: its location, capital and major cities, population, significant attractions, dominant religious groups, and major imports and exports. Then read up on its history and customs. Through internet pictures and videos, visit old towns and modern architecture, tranquil landscapes and joyous festivals. Bon voyage!

9 *It's a Fact*

When facts disprove something you had always thought was true, let the old assumption go. Don't be afraid to admit that you had been wrong or were misinformed. Far from looking foolish, you'll be admired for your courage and willingness to accept the truth, no matter where it leads. Stay teachable!

10 *Your Pressure Points*

How do you handle yourself under pressure? Your reactions in emergencies and the things you say when you're flustered speak volumes about the kind of person you are. If your pressure points push your buttons in all the wrong ways, practice skills that will help you respond to tense situations with poise and composure.

11 *It's a Celebration!*

Take time to celebrate how far you've come! Name the milestones you've passed, the big ideas you've had, and what you've learned, experienced, and accomplished over the last decade or two. It all has worked to bring you to the place you are now. But don't stop with history! Think ahead to where you'd like to go, and celebrate your future, too!

12

Take Eggstra Care!

If your list of pet peeves is long, it's likely that many people are walking on eggshells when they're around you. Which means they feel that they can't be themselves or express their thoughts for fear of causing offense. Make sure you haven't paved the ground around you with a thick layer of ready-to-crack eggshells! Laugh off petty annoyances. Decide that you aren't going to be easily irritated.

13

Be a Friend

You treat your friends well, but how do you treat yourself? If critical eyes meet you every time you look in the mirror and harsh words pepper your conversations with yourself, start looking at yourself the way you do your friends. After all, you're the closest one you have!

14

Make it Easier

Wouldn't it be great to finish all your day's to-do's and then completely relax tomorrow? But that's not always possible, and it's not desirable if it forces you to do your work carelessly or haphazardly. Reschedule what you can for tomorrow. You'll find both days are easier on your nerves—and you'll probably end up with a little kick-back time, too!

15 *Way of Speaking*

Know the difference between a rant and lively conversation. A rant requires only one person. It accepts agreement only and leaves no room for questions, much less dissent or another point of view. A lively conversation takes two or more who know how to balance speaking with listening. Agreement, disagreement, and concessions take place, all with respect for the other's humanity and intelligence.

16 *It's a Leap*

To make any progress, sometimes you just have to leap long and high! There's no halfway point that would let you stop, reconsider, and go back to exactly where you started. Think hard before making an irreversible decision. How will this benefit you? Get advice from trusted friends. Pray about it. And if you decide you're going to leap, give it all you've got!

17 *For the Future*

As we age, long-held character traits become etched into our personality. Often, several gain dominance, and we're more of what we've always been. Prepare for the future in the best way by being kind, generous, gentle, forgiving, patient, and lighthearted now. It will serve you well today, and it promises a happy tomorrow filled with continued warmth, love, and friendship!

18 *Take an Interest*

Don't settle for merely voicing your opinion. Get involved with causes, ideas, and topics that interest you. It's more rewarding to put your time and effort toward changing one thing for the better than talking and complaining about all the things that are wrong with the world. Life is not a spectator sport!

19 *You're the MVP*

It's one thing to have potential as, say, a tennis great, and quite another to do something about it. Up your game by doing all you can to develop, broaden, and strengthen the talents and abilities you possess. Do what it takes to become the star player God made you to be!

20 *There's a Beauty*

You can spend a fortune trying to get beautiful–or you can be beautiful for free! Immerse your heart and mind in kind, loving, and gentle thoughts about yourself, others, and the universe. When your inward thoughts are beautiful, your face shines with contentment, your words are permeated with understanding, and your actions are full of grace and purpose. Now there's a beauty!

21 *Seasons of Life*

Your life, like nature, has its rhythms and seasons. Embrace each as they come to you. Resistance pits you in a losing battle with reality, while acceptance frees you to let go of the past and discover all the present has to offer. You might discover more satisfaction, contentment, and fulfillment than you ever thought possible!

22 *Your Own Person*

Your associations–family, friends, neighbors, colleagues–shape the kind of person you are. Their values, customs, and habits influence yours more than you might realize. Be responsible for your own identity by not falling into behaviors and ways of thinking that go against your principles and the person you want to be.

23 *A Painful Reminder*

Ouch! That's the way your shoulders feel if you've been humped over a computer for hours on end. Or how your conscience feels when what you're saying and doing isn't in sync with what you know is right. Ouchies are indicators that something needs your attention–now. A good stretch might ease the shoulders. A little you-and-God time might settle your thoughts.

24 *Hey, It's Open!*

When a door slams shut in front of us, we often become so intent on trying to pick its lock that we never look up and see that three other doors are standing wide open, welcome mats out! Don't let the disappointment of one lost opportunity hide others that may prove more rewarding for you in the long run.

25 *All You've Got*

When you're faced with a challenging situation, give it all you've got. Do the best you can with what you have, and then let it go. It's useless to spend time second-guessing yourself or fretting over what might happen, because the outcome is no longer in your hands. You have done everything within your power to do, and that is success.

26 *Free to Be*

Many of our inhibitions serve a good purpose! Example: Someone lacking a filter between impulse and action is apt to lead a very tumultuous life. But other inhibitions keep us from freely delighting in the blessings of life and embracing opportunities God sends our way. When you feel your inhibitions are holding you back, stop and consider what they're holding you from.

27 *A Savvy Substitution*

When you see an item that you would love to own but can't afford to buy, ask yourself what attracts you about it. Is it design, style, functionality, beauty? For example, maybe it's the glitz of those designer shoes that you like, but you don't care about the designer name. Once you know what the real attraction is, look for a more affordable pair that satisfies your heart's desire.

28 *Face the Music*

Symphonic music is often built around a refrain, or motif. It appears throughout the piece, often in various forms as the composer expands and develops the theme. What do you see as a recurring motif in your life? Perhaps it's a certain way you approach various circumstances or handle different situations. Is it a motif worth repeating and enhancing, or would you like to change your tune?

29 *Secret of Contentment*

When it comes to possessions, "just one more" keeps you in a constant state of acquisition. When your attention is captured by what you want to get, you aren't seeing, much less enjoying, what you already possess. Tomorrow is bound to bring you what you need, so don't worry about it. For today, take delight in what you have.

30 *Know Your Limit*

A little stress can give you just the energy-boost you need to take care of what must get done today. It might even trigger a creative way to make one of those have-to's easier! But stress day after day can get so familiar that it becomes your normal feeling. That's an energy-zapper you don't want! Know how much stress works for you–and for how long.

May

1 *A Sensible Test*

It's been said that common sense is anything but common! When you have what seems like a fail-safe plan, hear what sounds like a no-fail proposition, or see a win-win situation, give it the common-sense test. It doesn't take brilliance, just an objective eye and the willingness to step back and ask a few questions. Does that make sense?

2 *Dress to Express*

If you dress to impress other people, you're hiding behind your clothes. You want others to see you as someone, deep down inside, you know you're really not. Keeping up an image drains your energy, diminishes your confidence, and prevents others from getting to know the real you. Let your personal presentation express who you are today and reflect your authentic self.

3 *A Perfect Idea*

Beauty and perfection aren't always found in the same place. A vase may be beautiful, yet chipped in places. A quilt may be beautiful without all the blocks and points in perfect alignment. Think twice before striving for your perfect self. All you'll get are some perfect worry wrinkles! Despite flaws–or maybe because of them–you are nothing short of beautiful!

4 *Stay in Control*

Most life events lie far outside your control. Other people are understandably resistant to being controlled by someone else. But God has given you control over yourself. You can control your reaction to what happens each day. You can control your response to the people who surround you. For peace of heart and mind, know what you can control–and what you cannot.

5 *Something to Hear*

You might not like what you hear, but don't shut your ears to it. Listen, and then weigh what was said against objective facts, your feelings and values, and the opinions of others. Maybe the comment is worth nothing more than a dismissive chuckle, but again, maybe it's a difficult truth that you really, really should take to heart.

6 *Take it Slow*

When a large sea-going vessel enters a harbor, it slows down. If it didn't, its wake would threaten, if not capsize, any smaller craft nearby. Similarly, the decisions you make affect those around you. Before going full-steam-ahead with a significant change of plans, consider the wake you will be leaving behind. Slow down! If it's life-changing for you, it's probably life-changing for others, too.

7 *An Emotional Appeal*

Your emotions are real. They may be intense and all-consuming. They may lift you to the heights of ecstasy or plunge you into the depths of hopelessness. They are also notoriously fickle! Acknowledge your emotions, but don't accept them as the whole story. Balance feelings with reason for a truer picture of where you are right now.

8 *Impressed and Inspired*

When you're doing the right thing, there's usually someone who will tell you it's the wrong thing! Perhaps because you are living your ideals, but she is not...and knows it. Maybe because you are sticking with your values, but he left his behind long ago...and feels it. Don't try to justify yourself. Your actions have made an impression that means more than any words could say.

9 *Take Little Steps*

Long-held habits are hard to break! When resolution after resolution hasn't worked for you, try mini resolutions. Say you're spending too much time on social media: shorten your viewing by ten minutes every few days. Or want to eat healthier meals: make one healthy serving substitution every week. Or would like to make meditation more a part of your life: gradually increase the minutes you meditate each day.

10 *Smell the Roses*

Never get so busy, so immersed in work, volunteerism, or online activities, that you have no time for anything else! While the things you do give your life purpose and pleasure, your inner self yearns to take a breather, listen to music, explore the world around you, and connect with friends face-to-face often. Remember to stop and smell the roses!

11 *Lot to Know*

The older you get, the wiser you get...but let's not take this and run with it! Remember that others, too, have had their share of life experiences. They, too, have met and overcome challenges which may not be readily apparent to you. Share what you know, and then prepare to know even more by listening!

12 *Laugh-A-Day*

How long has it been since you've had a good laugh? If it's been any longer than a day, you need more humor in your life! Okay, so maybe there's not much to laugh at right now, but there's plenty to pick from on websites devoted to jokes, anecdotes, witticisms, and humorous stories. In fact, you can probably sign up to have a giggle delivered to your inbox right now!

13 *Not All Bad!*

Bad days aren't all bad! A serious misstep compels us to rethink our behavior. A huge disappointment forces us to choose between despair or resilience. Personal loss pulls us deep into ourselves, and that's where God dwells. Even a bad hair day might prompt us to go for an easy-to-keep style that requires less fuss and shortens the morning routine by a good fifteen minutes!

14 *Too Much Giving?*

Yes, there's such a thing as being too generous! That's when you all too readily give away your time to anyone who asks. Or surrender your values when they don't prove popular, or hand over your self-confidence to whomever comes along with a critical remark. Claim what is yours! There are some things that aren't meant to be given away!

15 *Savor the Moment*

A personal tragedy grabs our attention in a way that nothing else can. Suddenly, what we had taken for granted is no longer there. Our worries, concerns, and daily activities fall away to nothing, because now we're focused on something much more important. Don't wait for a life-changing event to teach you to savor every precious moment of your day!

16 *Grab Your Happiness*

What makes you happy? What lifts your heart and makes you smile? It's probably not some grand event or big-ticket purchase, but something simple, something ordinary, something small. Maybe seeing a vase of yellow flowers sitting on your desk, touching the cashmere throw draped over your chair, hearing your favorite song, licking a chocolate ice cream cone. Once you know what makes you happy, fill your life with happiness!

17 *Time of Peace*

Maybe you don't see big changes looming on your horizon right now. Good, but don't let peaceful routine morph into a mind-numbing rut. Devote your time and attention to the business of daily living. Notice your surroundings, appreciate your everyday blessings, and perhaps make a few of those little personal changes you've been thinking about lately.

18 *Pearl of Wisdom*

It's an irritant–perhaps a grain of sand–that produces a pearl inside an oyster. From a piece of grit comes a lovely and precious bead! In our lives, too, irritants cause change. Unlike the oyster, however, we can decide what emerges–bitterness or energy, resentment or creativity, a bigger and grittier grain of sand or an astoundingly beautiful pearl!

19 *A Good Host*

Sometimes hosts get so occupied with pouring beverages and passing plates that a pleasant evening for guests is an exhausting ordeal for her! If you obsess about the comfort, happiness, and well-being of everyone else in your life, perhaps it's time to think about the kind of "host" you are to yourself. Take time to sip your tea, nibble a tidbit, and actually enjoy the people around you!

20 *Check It Out*

How do you feel? Your physician will ask, but don't wait until your next check-up to answer the question. Identify your deepest needs that are rarely put into words unless you ask. Admit that what you heard someone say bothered you instead of letting it go unaddressed. Be attentive to the way you really feel, and act on it in the most positive and productive way.

21 *Be a Friend*

Just as you love to be around the people who make you feel comfortable, relaxed, and happy, return the favor. Be a loving, caring presence in their lives by giving them your full attention, marking with them their joys and successes, consoling them in their sorrows, and encouraging them in their dreams and aspirations. Be the kind of friend you love to have around!

22 *Just One Commitment*

It's better to commit yourself to one thing and do it well than to take on many and do them half-heartedly. In choosing one, you're showing a realistic assessment of your time and abilities, and demonstrating your willingness to give it your undivided attention and effort. With that, you're more than likely to find fulfillment in the process and feel happy with the outcome!

23 *Eyes Wide Open*

Good leaders know that what they do is far more persuasive than what they say. They look to high principles to guide them, because, as the adage says, "Actions speak louder than words." Good followers watch with a discerning eye. They know that they, as individuals, are ultimately responsible for what they do, so they never follow blindly. Sometimes you lead and sometimes you follow. Do both with eyes wide open!

24 *Some Respectable Advice*

Self-respect enables you to uphold your beliefs and values, even if others mock or ignore them. It lets you keep your head high, despite circumstances that threaten to tear you down. Self-respect is like a ray of light at the center of your being that grows brighter and stronger as you treasure it, practice it, and live by it. And when you respect yourself, respect for others comes naturally.

25

What a Blessing!

You're blessed to be blessed! Take a few minutes today to thank God for all your blessings—the people you love, the essentials you possess, the comforts you enjoy, the hopes that you cherish, the desires that you cradle in your heart. Thank Him for good memories, and thank Him in advance for all those yet to come. If you're blessed and you know it, give thanks!

26

It's an Honor

Allow yourself the honor of doing a favor for someone who cannot repay you. A full bag of dry goods to the local food pantry...a donation of clean, gently used, and nicely folded clothes to a thrift shop...a helping hand to a stranger who needs assistance managing stairs, opening doors, reaching merchandise displayed on a high shelf. It may be the most rewarding moment of your day!

27

Cultivate a Trait

If you wish you were more confident, more patient, more energetic, more enthusiastic, more charismatic—what's holding you back? Challenge yourself by cultivating the character trait you want to possess. Imagine yourself with it. Act like you have it. It might feel a little fake when you start out, but little by little, you'll get it. And you'll know you're a natural the first time someone admires it in you!

28 *How It's Done*

Just because you've always done it that way, does it still work? Is it still as efficient and effective, or is an upgrade in order? Whether it's a recently adopted celebration or a long-held family tradition, a daily task or a whole way of thinking about yourself, others, and the world, ask the question. If it survives scrutiny, keep it up! But if not, it's probably time to do things differently.

29 *To Know You*

You'll never get to know yourself unless you spend time with yourself. That is, no electronic pings piquing your curiosity about what's happening out there when your focus is in here! No outside voices and inside whispers telling you what you should or shouldn't feel or think. In your busy, interconnected life, the most challenging person to get to know is yourself!

30 *Look At It*

Look to those ahead of you, because they have a lot to teach you. Look to those beside you, because they're walking hand-in-hand with you. Look to those behind you, because what you do has the power to teach and inspire them, encourage them and give them hope. Most of all, look to God above you because in His hands is the goodness of life itself.

May

31 *Think About It*

Do you know why you hear so much whining about what's wrong with the world? Because whining is easier than coming up with feasible ways of making things better! Save your words for good ideas and your energy for taking action. And if what's wrong with the world is beyond your control, steer your thoughts toward what's right with it–now you have a lot to think about!

June

1 *The Kindest Way*

If you need to have a difficult conversation with someone, you already know what you want to say. But plan how to say it. Pulling in a deep breath and letting all the words tumble out is the quickest way, but neither the kindest nor most effective. Speak gently, as if you're embracing, comforting, loving them. Your words will come carefully, but kindly–and with every chance of being heard.

2 *Call Them Angels*

Just as you pulled off the road with a flat tire, another driver stopped behind you and offered to fix it. The day you learned you would need a medical specialist, you heard that the best in the country had just opened a clinic nearby. The weekend you felt forgotten by the world, a childhood friend got in touch with you. Some call them coincidences. Others call them angels in disguise.

3 *At the Movies*

Dramatic scenes make riveting movies, but it's poor viewing in real life. Take time to examine what has really taken place. Does it warrant heightened emotions, breathless proclamations, and vivid predictions of doom? Probably not. But if the situation is serious, it needs your full attention, not a fit of hysteria. If you want edge-of-your-seat drama, catch it at a theater near you!

4 *Pros and Cons*

Before making a major shift in direction, consider the pros and cons. Staying where you are offers comfort, continuity, and lifelong connections, but not the opportunities you may find in a new place. Leaving provides exposure to wider experience, but takes you away from the place where you may have had deep roots. Think. Pray. And then embrace the decision you come to with all your heart!

5 *A Fresh Approach*

Stale bread makes a lackluster lunch. So do regrets, resentments, grudges, and rivalries. If you're still chewing on what happened in years gone by, your mind is too full to savor new relationships, new ideas, and new interests. To avoid waste, maybe you'll go ahead and finish that week-old loaf of bread, but pitch feelings and stories that have been around way too long. Start each day fresh!

6

Talk About Talking

The words you use when you speak about others have a way of sticking to you. Though snarky remarks may get a laugh at someone else's expense, they come at your expense, too. Your hearers are bound to think, "I'll keep my distance–it's them now, but it could be me next!" You heard it in kindergarten: If you can't say something nice, don't say anything at all.

7

Courage to Accept

When your plans don't seem to be coming together, remember that there's a higher Power whose plans are beyond anything you can see right now. Go along with what you must, even if you don't know yet where it is taking you. At times, humble acceptance takes more courage than stubborn insistence on getting your own way.

8

Remember Your Priorities

If your calendar is crammed full of daily have-to's and want-to's, you're headed toward burnout. While all your activities may be worthwhile, you cannot make all of them priorities, or at least at this point in your life. Look at your day's list and see what you can delegate, save for later, or eliminate. Why? Because your physical and emotional well-being is your top priority!

9

Class in Character

Thank those who pull you aside and confront you with what you are doing wrong. While you're bound to feel sheepish when it happens, they're giving you a chance to turn things around. Plus, the experience may save you from a much more serious mistake later. Some of our best teachers are those who are willing to call us as they see us!

10

Sunny Side Up

Lighten up! A sense of humor keeps your heart lighter, releasing it from the weight of anger and bitterness. It opens the window to a sunnier outlook on life, a perspective more likely to notice a sparkle than a slight, the funny side than the gloomy side. When your sense of humor shines through, the brighter your world–and the world of everyone around you!

11

Now's Your Time!

We often get so caught up in planning for and working toward the next stage in life that we forget to enjoy the one we're in! Yes, your dreams, goals, and objectives give what you're doing today meaning and purpose, but there will never be another today. Make the most of it! Savor the joy of being who you are and where you are. At every time, make it the best time of your life!

12 *He's Got It!*

God is present, even when you don't feel it. He is ready to hear you, whether you have pain or praise, sorrow or laughter, unease or contentment to share with Him. If you need something, ask Him, even if you can't find the words to express your inmost thoughts and desires. Experience for yourself the joy and the freedom of knowing with all your heart, "God's got this!"

13 *Resign Right Now!*

"I was a lot happier," someone once remarked, "when I resigned from managing the universe!" Take a tip from the quipster. Help when you can and advise when you're asked, but let adults solve their own problems. There are things even God chooses not to micro-manage, and that's His gift of human choice!

14 *God Loves Knee-Mail*

You probably don't wait for something big to happen before you send a friend an email. No, email is an easy and convenient way to keep in touch, even if it's only a few lines about daily stuff. Prayer is even easier and more convenient–no electronic device needed! Only a day-to-day whisper of your heart turned to God, who's always there to listen.

15 *Lose Weight Instantly*

Worry is like a big bag of potato chips—once you reach into it, it's impossible to stop! Yet (and you know this) worry solves nothing. All it does is burden you with more worry. So hand the worry-bag over to God. With that out of the way, you're ready to tackle whatever it was you were worried about!

16 *Heart That Shows*

Do you hide your heart behind a facade of toughness, sophistication, defensiveness, or distrust? Any one of these could be a way of shielding your heart from hurt, or a desire to come across as someone you aren't. Be true to yourself. Let others see a heart filled with caring and compassion, tenderness and love—the heart God has in mind for you.

17 *Take Yourself Lightly*

It's been said that those who cannot laugh at themselves feel every bump in the road—and they do! Everyone makes an occasional silly mistake, embarrassing gaffe, or unfiltered remark. Honest acceptance of your own humanness allows you to laugh at yourself, set others at ease, and enjoy a smoother ride ahead!

18 *Life is Good*

Have you ever heard a phrase said so many times that you stop listening to it? "Have a good attitude" might be one that comes to mind. But consider this–it's repeated so many times because it's important. Taking on the day with an upbeat mindset helps you cope better and feel happier–and lightens the load for everyone around you, too!

19 *Believe in Yourself*

When your gut tells you something's wrong, something's probably wrong. When you have misgivings about what you're being asked to do, or when you feel pushed to go along with things despite your questions, set aside some God-and-me time to sort through your true feelings, hopes, and desires.

20 *Silence Is Golden*

Speaking up takes courage, but knowing when to keep quiet takes wisdom. Even truthful, valid, and helpful comments need to be heard by a receptive audience, or they are quickly ignored or dismissed. The right word at the right time and in the right ears can make the right difference in someone's life.

21

One Bright Point

When you're on the receiving end of kindness, you respond with kindness. But when someone's rude to you, you might be tempted to give it right back. Instead, meet rudeness with kindness. You never know what's going on in the person's life. Perhaps your smile will be the brightest point of their whole day!

22

Beyond Plan A

Sometimes the best-laid Plan A just doesn't work out. Things happen that you couldn't have foreseen, parts of the process took longer than expected, or people didn't come through as you thought they would. Don't let that stop you. Pause, regroup, and start on Plan B. And remember, there are 24 more letters in the alphabet left to use!

23

Appreciate the Present

Mindful living doesn't come naturally. We're prone to either ruminate ad nauseam about the past, or spend hour upon hour daydreaming about some future time when everything will be perfect. All the while, we're letting the present moment slip away, unnoticed, unseen, unappreciated. Today, live in the moment. Experience it. Savor it. Give thanks for it.

24

Renew, Discover, Bloom

When "same-old, same-old" becomes your standard answer to the question, "What did you do today?" it's time to step out of the rut. Take a break and do something different. See a movie you wouldn't normally see...go to an exotic restaurant...browse books at the library and pick one outside your go-to topics. It could take you to a whole new level of living!

25

All Wrapped Up

The only way people can get to know you is if you talk about your interests and activities. But equally important is how well you listen when they tell you what they're doing and share their thoughts and opinions. Make sure you leave an opening for the conversation to flow both ways. Remember, if you're all wrapped up in yourself, you're seriously overdressed!

26

Winning Isn't Everything

The hardest thing to give is in! Yet sometimes giving in frees you from a pointless argument that could lead to words you'll later regret, or even a ruptured relationship. Accept that the other person sees things differently. If necessary, discuss it later after emotions have cooled. But for now, graciously give in.

27

Make Your Breaks

If the door of opportunity isn't swinging open for you, oil the hinges. Take on a task or responsibility that needs doing. Devote yourself to the challenging training course that others shrink from taking. Volunteer in support of a cause you believe in. Give a relationship a chance to grow. Who knows what might open up to you?

28

Embrace God's Love

Although it's impossible to grasp the height, depth, and breadth of God's love for each one of us, His love is always there! Take a moment to sit back, close your eyes, and let it fill your heart, mind, and spirit. Pull in as much as you can manage. Wrapped in a great big God-hug, you'll feel head-to-toe loved all day long (because you are, you know)!

29

Tip the Scales

You can't control everything that goes on in your life–no one can! But there are little things you can do to make whatever is going on, go better. Embrace every day with a friendly smile, an optimistic outlook, realistic expectations, and a Thank-You-God prayer from your heart. Tip the scales in your favor!

30

Complete the Picture

Never judge a book by its cover, or a resort by its postcards! Sure, both glossy pictures look inviting, but you haven't seen enough to really decide whether you'd like to read the book or visit the resort. The same is true with people. First impressions can deceive. Get a more complete picture before you delve into a new relationship.

JULY

1 *Nuts to You!*

It's been said that God gives us the nuts, but He doesn't crack them for us. And when it comes to personal success, the toughest nuts to crack are the most worthwhile achievements. They're the "nuts" that take time and effort...demand diligence and commitment...require a willingness to explore and discover. In other words, for success in life, get cracking!

2 *Smile at You*

Chances are that you smile when you see the face of a friend or loved one. But what happens when you look at yourself in the mirror? Instead of frowning at your perceived flaws, look happy! The glow of a warm smile makes any face brighter, and it has a way of warming hearts, too–starting with your own!

3

Refuse the Blues

It's natural to feel sad after something bad has happened, but sometimes the blues simply come knocking. Don't offer them a chair! In fact, act as if they aren't even around. Read a few jokes, listen to upbeat music, do something you enjoy doing– before you know it, those down-in-the-dumps feelings have slipped out the back door.
Bye-bye, blues!

4

No More Measurements!

Compare yourself with no one else, and your life with none other. Instead, get so busy living that you have no time left to measure yourself against other people. Embrace your present age, relationships, and daily activities. Be proud of what's good, and work to improve what needs to improve. Share your time and resources with others, and let them look up to you!

5 *Yet To Be*

There's no joy in rehashing what might have been. Instead, consider what's yet to be. Think about what God may have in mind for you. No matter where the day leads you, it's bound to put you in touch with fresh ideas, new perspectives, and noteworthy adventures. For a joy-filled life, open yourself to what is to come!

6 *Do the Footwork*

"Overnight success" rarely happens overnight! Most often the "overnight success" has put in years of dedicated effort unseen by adoring fans. Everyone loves an overnight-success story, but the surest way to success in any endeavor is day-by-day commitment, constant practice, and hard work.

7 *Life is Risky!*

There's nothing you can do that isn't risky. Sure, if you step out of your comfort zone, you could risk failure. But if you never try anything new, you risk boredom and stagnation. You could initiate a friendship and risk rejection, or never reach out to others and risk overwhelming loneliness. Life is full of risks, so risk being happy, loved, and loving.

8 *Create Positive Change*

Nothing except God and His love for you remains unchanged throughout your lifetime. Throughout every season of life, take charge of change by focusing on the good that comes out of it, the new opportunities it opens up, and the maturity and insight it brings you. Even unwelcome, unexpected change can be the foundation of a positive experience.

9 *Be a Friend*

Ralph Waldo Emerson said, "The only way to have a friend is to be one." Be one to your long-time friends by remaining close to them and caring about them through all life's seasons. Be one to new friends by cultivating shared interests and activities. You'll not only be the best kind of friend, but you'll have the best kind of friends around you!

10 *When Money Talks*

How you manage your money is telling on you! It reveals how much you're willing to spend on possessions, status, and bragging rights. It shows whether you're more apt to indulge your wants or help the needy. It displays your values when you either spend it all now, or save some for a rainy day. What is your money saying about you?

11

Stop for Fuel

During a long road trip, you're likely to stop periodically to refuel your vehicle and grab a bite to eat. You might even spend a few minutes relaxing before you're ready to hit the road again. On a busy day, don't forget your rest stops. A little time out for fuel and renewal will keep you going longer and stronger!

12

Dismiss the Doubters

When you share your hopes and plans with others, there's usually someone who fills your ears with dire warnings. Listen, but only long enough to evaluate whether you're hearing wise advice or negative nitpicking. Heed the one, but dismiss the other with nothing more than a nod and a smile.

13 *Loads of Laughter*

Sometimes you have to get serious, but not all the time! Make time for tickly giggles and goofy antics. Daydream and dawdle a while. It's relaxing and heart-lifting, calming and joy-building. And then, when you can't escape the cares of the world, you'll come at them with a much happier, healthier perspective–and maybe with a few good ideas to solve them, too!

14 *For Feet's Sake*

If you want to forget your troubles, wear tight shoes! Aching feet have a way of capturing your attention, just as any one problem can take over all your thoughts and attention. Define what's bothering you. Maybe you'll need someone to help you with it. Or maybe it's just a matter of taking off your shoes!

15 *Act on It*

An impulse to visit a friend...call on a neighbor... help a stranger...initiate a conversation with someone you've never met before. Though God plants seeds like this in your mind, He doesn't make them bloom. That's for you to do! The next time a God-seed sprouts in you, nurture it. God plants the seed, and you get to share the fragrant flowers!

16 *Dress for Success*

What you're wearing tells something about you, but even more telling is how you wear it. An air of haughty self-importance can cheapen even the most elegant gown. An attitude of acceptance, humility, and graciousness makes well-worn jeans and a comfortable top look like a million dollars. Search your heart, not your closet, if you want to wear the best.

17

Try Something New

As teens, we care deeply what others think about us. After ten years or so, we shield ourselves from criticism by claiming that we don't care what others think. Only later in life do we realize that few people were thinking about us at all–they were too busy thinking about themselves! Don't let self-consciousness hold you back. Go ahead and do what you've always wanted to do!

18

Enjoy the Walk

Do you love a mystery? Consider the magnificent mystery of your spiritual walk. As you rely on a good writer to put all the pieces together at the end, trust God to faithfully lead you, even though you don't have all the answers right now Enjoy your story–the good read of a lifetime!

19

Never Too Late

Sometimes it is too late! Say we may not have had the opportunity to become a star basketball player when we were young, but we can cheer on our favorite team, interest others in the sport, and maybe even get a driveway game going with the neighbors. It's never too late to give your time, effort, and support to what you've always loved!

20

Give It Away

When you do a favor for a friend, make it a real favor–the kind that expects nothing in return. In fact, forget you even did it! Then, when your friend returns the kindness, it will come as a surprise and delight rather than payment due.

21

Make Your Choices

It's easy to go with the flow, but be careful–the current might take you where you don't want to end up! When you're among others, make sure their choices are also your choices. If you have misgivings, it might be time for you to step out of the water and chart your own course.

22 *Simplify, Simplify, Simplify!*

A gazillion ideas whirling around your mind make it impossible to focus on any one thought. It's like looking at a shelf so jam-packed with knick-knacks and bric-a-brac that no one item stands out. Close your eyes and consciously clear your mind, and then give your attention to one idea at a time. You'll feel calmer–and think smarter.

23 *Life Saving Treatment*

Never nurse a grudge. Grudges do nothing more than invite anger and misery into the core of your being–a far worse consequence than anything you could deal out to the person who offended you. Instead, sincerely and completely forgive the person. Ask God to help you do so. It's not easy, but it's heart-freeing and life-saving.

24 *Live It Up!*

When outward circumstances or inner emotions threaten to drag you down, think "up" instead. Lift your eyes to God, thanking Him for the blessings you enjoy right now. Raise your thoughts to productive solutions, and dismiss all-is-lost imaginings. Boost your mood with upbeat music, dancing for the joy of it. When you're down, don't stay there–live it up!

25 *Add the Sprinkles*

Icing for cake...whipped cream for pie...fudge for ice cream...yum! But why not make it sparkle with a dash of sprinkles? Only a little extra touch moves a dessert from good to super-good, from "aaaah" to "wow"! In everything you do, with everything you are, give it the sprinkle treatment–a little extra effort is all it takes!

26 *Load-Sharing Plan*

Is your calendar crammed with to-do's? Manage your time (and keep your sanity) by delegating what you can. Let others pick up part of the load. Tasks might not get done exactly the way you would like, but they'll get done–and maybe even a tad better. Remember that many hands make light work!

27

So They Say

Gossip has always run fast, but now it travels at supersonic speed! But that doesn't mean it's true or even half-true. Before making up your mind about someone who's the subject of gossip, meet them as a person God loves dearly. Perhaps you are the one He is asking to extend His compassion and care to a hurt and sorrowing heart.

28

Get the Message

Some days you just don't want to get out of bed. Your body's message: You need a break. Perhaps you've been so caught up with taking care of others that you need a few hours to yourself. When you can, take some time off to relax. A luxury spa would be idyllic, but a nice long evening at home works just as well (and it's much easier on your wallet)!

29 *Let Him Know*

Important people in your life get to hear how much they mean to you, don't they? Although they already know, everyone likes to hear words of love and praise, appreciation and gratitude. God already knows, too, but isn't it nice once in a while to lift your eyes to the sky and tell Him how much He means and how thankful you are for all He does?

30 *The Little Things*

In homes, businesses, churches, and communities, some work goes unnoticed–until it's not done. It's only then that the family member who folds the laundry, janitor who cleans the building, woman who makes the coffee, or neighbor who sweeps the sidewalk is truly appreciated. Today, thank someone who takes care of "little" things that make the day go smoothly. Let them know you notice!

JULY

31 *The Big Picture*

How frustrating to near the end of a jigsaw puzzle only to realize that several pieces are missing! Yet your life is full of unanswered questions, bewildering mysteries, unclear direction–in other words, missing pieces. These are pieces God holds in His hand. Trust Him, because He knows what the big picture looks like!

AUGUST

1 *Check the Baggage*

What a relief to finally turn over that heavy suitcase to the airport porter! You feel as if you've shed fifty pounds, you can stand up straight again, and you can walk with a spring in your step. It's not far from how you feel inside when you get rid of past defeats and nagging regrets. Check 'em with God, and leave 'em forever!

2

A Blessed Day

Some people hope for blessings. Others take matters into their own hands–they make blessings happen. Choose an optimistic outlook, and you'll bless yourself with good cheer, gratitude, and a sense of confidence and self-worth. And when you feel good about you, you're bound to find a wealth of blessings in your every day.

3

Have It All

What does it take to have it all? If reaching the pinnacle of success at work or amassing a fortune comes to mind, you're straining for the horizon. But if you love what you're doing and you're content with what you have, you have it all today. Whether more or less comes your way in the future, you will always have it all.

4

The Leading Edge

If you're attracted to a certain profession, get your foot in the door by volunteering. You'll meet people working in the field you're interested in–it's natural networking. Once you're known as a proactive, capable, and reliable person, you've got the lead when it comes to hiring decisions. In fact, they'll come knocking at your door instead of the other way around!

5 *Story to Tell*

Everyone you meet has a story to tell, but all too often no one asks them to tell it. Yet other people's backgrounds, experiences, hopes, thoughts, ideas, and perspectives can enhance your life in many ways. To deepen your relationships, increase your understanding, expand your worldview, and broaden your knowledge of life, all you need to do is ask.

6 *Work in Progress*

"Even a stopped clock is right twice a day!" The proverb serves as a cautionary tale to those who want nothing less than personal perfection. They're in for a lifetime of disappointment. Have patience with yourself, and do the best you can every day. While making improvements, remember that no one is perfect. Everyone is a work in progress!

7 *Person of Influence*

Whenever you're around other people, you're making an impression on them. They pick up on your attitude, just as you do theirs. Your friendly smile and relaxed, comfortable-with-yourself demeanor sets others at ease and goes a long way to promote a pleasant, welcoming atmosphere all around. Use your influence today!

8 *A New Day*

Start each day afresh. Leave yesterday's stumbles, regrets, disappointments, and shortcomings behind–wipe the slate clean! Give your time, effort, and attention to making progress from where you are right now. With good choices, smart decisions, and heavenly guidance, begin today!

9 *Calorie-Free Concoction*

The not-so-nice quip on the tip of the tongue. The angry words that come to mind. Beware! Once you say something, you can't unsay it. The moment a remark makes its way out of your mouth, you have no control over how it's taken or to whom it's repeated. Sometimes it's hard to not say what you're thinking, but remember: swallowed words are completely calorie-free!

10 *Don't Be Afraid*

What are you afraid to do? If you're afraid, say, to scamper across a busy street against a red light, good! Well-founded fear works in your favor. But if you're afraid to do something new simply because it's outside your comfort zone, then fear is keeping you on too short of a leash. Break loose, be brave, and give it a try!

11 *Make Some Space*

Your calendar is way too crowded if it's filled with back-to-back appointments and meetings. Whenever possible, put some space between obligations to allow for unexpected delays. And if there's no delay, great–you have a few extra minutes to sit back, relax, and maybe even catch a little catnap!

12 *Congrats to You!*

If you need a boost today, name your proudest achievements so far. While some may have earned recognition, like winning a spelling bee in school or getting a promotion at work, others are private ones that make your heart grin–like baking a picture-perfect batch of cookies or figuring out how to navigate that new app on your phone. Congratulate yourself, because you've earned it!

13 *Wish I May*

Maybe you harbor a wish that you've long since decided will never happen. Of course it won't if you never do anything practical about it! Share your secret wish with God. Perhaps a way to move on the idea will occur to you. Or you'll realize that there are more realistic and ultimately more rewarding choices open to you.

14 *Here and Now*

You're working toward your goal–perhaps it's an advanced degree, a workplace promotion, a healthier body, increased emotional stability, financial security. Keep up the good work! Meanwhile, don't let the pleasures of the present moment slip past you. Embrace and enjoy who you are, where you are, and what you have right now.

15 *A Winding Road*

Life's road isn't a straight highway from one point to the next. You go through hills and valleys, around turns and curves, and in unexpected and surprising directions. It's said that those who get the most out of the journey are those who can enjoy the scenery, even when they're on a detour. Are you one of them?

16 *Determine to Grow*

We have to admire the determination of weeds. Despite layers of mulch or rock, weeds manage to wiggle their way up from ground to the garden. Are you courageous enough, and determined enough, to keep growing despite the obstacles? Maybe that's why someone once quipped, "Lord, give me the tenacity of a weed!"

17 *Spread the Smiles*

Some things are meant to be shared. Like a bowl of candy and a batch of cookies. An enjoyable book, a heartwarming story, a laugh-out-loud joke, a helpful tip, and a hearty compliment. Laughter, too, is one of those things. Why keep it to yourself?
Spread the smiles!

18 *A Timely Tip*

After all is said and done...well, all too often there's more said than done, isn't there? When you take on a project or assume a position, spend minimal time elaborating on your qualifications and what you plan to do, and maximum time doing everything you said you would do.

19 *Clear for Takeoff!*

Take a lesson from an airplane. It takes off against the wind! What's working against you might be exactly what you need for flight. When the winds aren't with you, don't be afraid to keep pushing. Later, when you're soaring, you might look back and realize how much those contrary winds were working for you all along!

20 *Advice Not Taken*

Many people are happy to serve God–but only in an advisory capacity! You feel you know what you need better than He. You know exactly how a problem could be–should be!–solved, but then God comes along with something completely different. Stand back, take a deep breath, and let God be God.

21 *Set Daily Goals*

Establish a long-term objective, and set day-to-day objectives for yourself. While remaining flexible enough to take advantage of options and opportunities that open along the way, specific, achievable daily goals give your activities meaning and purpose. They work to keep you headed toward where you want to go.

22 *One Small Step*

There's nothing wrong with reaching for the stars as long as you keep your feet on the ground. Dream big, but don't let your dreams carry you away from reality. One small, practical, genuine achievement will do more to lift you star-ward than talking about a dazzling array of lofty fantasies.

23 *The Bright Side*

Here's a game for you. The next time you're facing an unwelcome circumstance, challenge yourself to come up with at least one good thing about it. Name three things, and you're a winner! Your upbeat attitude will do more than anything else to get you through a bad situation. Besides, when you're looking on the bright side, you never have to worry about eye strain!

24 *In Good Character*

The woman who risks losing her job for the sake of exposing dishonesty has character, no doubt about it. But so does the one who works hard and conscientiously whether the boss is present or not. Who submits honest and accurate financial records. Who speaks well of others in keeping with the truth. Day-to-day character counts.

25 *That Little Extra*

Perhaps you know someone who always puts that extra "oomph!" into whatever she's doing. She gives the present moment her full attention, and shows genuine enthusiasm for her work. The task itself might be something we'd call menial or routine, but she's not one to wait until the big break comes along before she delights in life. Does this describe you?

26 *Still Small Voice*

The time you spend in spiritual reflection is time well spent. It allows you to connect with your real feelings, and perhaps even discern that "still small voice" inside you and what it's saying. Perhaps a solution to a problem...a whisper of warning...a perspective you hadn't thought of before. You'll want to hear it.

27 *We're a Team!*

There's no such thing as a one-woman show. Even alone on the stage, she's there thanks to parents, teachers, coaches, and mentors. Audience applause is also thanks to stagehands, lighting technicians, make-up artists, costumers, script writers, prompters–and the crew that built the theater.

28 *Just for You*

Isn't it great to receive an invitation from your BFF to see a movie...go out to eat...or just get together for an evening chatfest? No special occasion needed! Every day, God has an invitation for you. It's called prayer. No major issue required. He likes to hear about the small stuff, the nitpicky snags, and all the ho-hum happenings of an ordinary day.

29 *Expect the Good*

If you expect trouble, you're sure to get it, right? The same can be said for things at the opposite end of the spectrum. Expect kindness of others, and you're more than likely to receive it. Expect opportunities to arise, and you'll start finding them. Expect beauty in the course of an ordinary day, and you'll see it. Yes, expect the good!

August

30 *To "No" Yourself*

To know yourself is also to "no" yourself. That's the willingness to tell yourself "no" when your desires, emotions, or ambitions start crossing the line. When you can say "no" to words and actions that could put you in harm's way, compromise your reputation, or trample the rights of others means you're saying "yes" to personal pride and self-respect.

31 *Keep Your Head*

If you can keep your head when all about you is losing theirs...you might not understand the problem! Or maybe you do. But instead of responding to passionate rhetoric, you've done the research, uncovered the real issues, and now can separate reasoned argument from groundless fears. When emotions are hot, keep a cool head–and use it.

September

1 *Who Will Decide?*

Sometimes you get to the end of a day and feel completely discouraged. Someone let you down big time...you didn't get what seemed like a sure thing a short time ago...you've jumped through all the hoops with little to show for it. Sigh! But don't let discouragement decide your attitude. Resolve to start tomorrow with renewed strength, courage, and confidence.

2 *Humble Hearts Share*

Connect with others by telling them about your activities and expertise, but speak from a humble heart. Share what you believe might be a mutual interest, or an accomplishment of yours that you think might draw out the other person. Genuine humility neither boasts nor hides behind a veil of false modesty.

3 *A Little Nut*

Have you ever seen a 100-year-old oak tree? Over the decades, it has withstood ferocious storms and intense lightning. Possibly drenching rains, years of drought, freezing winters, and scorching summers. And how about the forest fire that once charred its topmost branches? Every mighty oak is here today because yesterday's little nut was determined to keep on growing!

4 *Heart of Love*

When a difficult person is part of your life, equip yourself with good coping strategies. It helps to remember that they are, like you, a dear child of God. Respond to their negative words and actions with a heart of compassion and love. It will help you retain your composure and peace of mind. And who knows? They might start to follow your example some day!

5 *It Can Happen*

While personal experience teaches valuable lessons, there are some lessons best learned second-hand. When someone suffers the consequences of his or her own ill-advised decisions or reckless actions, never think, "It couldn't happen to me." No one is immune from the natural and inevitable laws of cause and effect.

6 *Catch the Bug!*

One person's cold gets transferred from person to person to person, rippling out like rings from a stone thrown in a pond. One person's kindness works in the same way. Who knows how many days will be brightened, how many hearts will be lifted, because of your single act of contagious kindness today?

7 *Gather the Good*

Go back through your life and pick out all the good things that have happened to you. Recall the people who encouraged you, who made you feel accomplished, confident, and valued. List the skills and achievements that make you proud. Before you're finished, you'll realize that you have a lot to be thankful for–a whole lot!

8

Is It True?

"A lie will go around the world while truth is pulling its boots on." The adage, often attributed to Mark Twain, points out how quickly a colorful fabrication gets passed from one person to another. Its emotional appeal and intriguing details draw listeners like moths to a glowing lightbulb. Don't get burnt by clicking and sharing without checking first!

9

Moments of Delight

Aren't happy surprises delightful? Say, getting a call from a long-lost childhood friend who dug until she found you...opening your backdoor and seeing the upturned face of the beloved puppy you thought had wandered away...finding that little stash of cash in your billfold that you had long forgotten. Smile for every delightful moment, and relive it often!

10

Can of Success

Did you know that success comes in cans? It does when failure comes in can'ts! Question the can't that holds you back. Is it real or imagined? Does it emanate from lack of confidence or an actual personal or situational limitation? What skill, help, or knowledge would work to change can't to can? This time, open the "can" and see what's in it!

11

Day's Best Decision

The most rewarding, life-enhancing decision you can make today is a decision to be happy. Happiness makes good times even better and not-so-good times less stressful, because you know the difficulties are not your whole reality. And the sense of humor that springs from a happy heart can turn a challenging situation into a genuinely funny one!

12

Fully In Sync

Who you are when no one's looking measures your authenticity. Honesty in private makes honesty so much a part of you that someone's underhanded suggestion never has a chance. Unseen kindnesses become such a habit that there's never a moment's pause between you and a thoughtful act when you're with others. Authenticity means that private behavior and public conduct are fully in sync!

13 *Today and Tomorrow*

Although no one can predict the future, you can prepare for it by making the best use of today. Good work habits, a balanced and healthy lifestyle, a joyful attitude, and sound spiritual principles that you practice now will put you on course to successfully meet whatever tomorrow may bring.

14 *Tell Me Why*

"How did this happen to me?" It's a cry every heart has raised, and usually more than once. God seldom provides a clear, direct reply that would sound reasonable to human ears. Rather than demand an answer, acknowledge your new reality. Humble acceptance, along with trust in God's power and goodness, will see you through life's difficult times.

15 *Sit and Think*

How long has it been since you've taken time out to simply sit and think? If it's been a while, do it now. Turn off the phone and computer, get a mug of coffee, and find a spot where you can mull over whatever's going on. By the time your mug is empty, your day will look much brighter–and you'll feel a whole lot better, too!

16 *It's Good Enough*

Perfectionism is like living with 30-pound weights around your ankles. Everything becomes slow and laborious because it has to come out perfectly, no matter how insignificant the task at hand. Give your best effort to the things that matter. For everything else, know when good enough is good enough.

17 *Keep on Track*

"Even if you're on the right track," noted humorist Will Rogers, "you'll get run over if you just sit there." Even the best plans require daily, practical steps forward if they're to become reality. Even if your steps are small, keep moving toward your goal!

18 *Love Is Patient*

When you practice patience, you do yourself a favor. You avoid stress and anger while standing in a slow-moving line...waiting for a green light...sitting on-hold as minutes tick by. You do others a favor as well, because your good humor is contagious, your law-abiding driving keeps everyone safe, and you won't forget to speak kindly when you reach a customer service agent!

19

The First Question

If a friend or neighbor asks you to do a favor for them, you're apt to say yes. That's good–but even better is to do it before they have a chance to ask. Take time to notice what someone might need and how you might be able to lend a hand. Then it's you with the first question: "May I help?"

20

God's Anatomy Lesson

It has long been noted that we have two ears and only one mouth. Perhaps this is an on-your-face nudge from God reminding us to focus less on what we have to tell others and more on hearing what others have to tell us. We can never hope to understand the concerns, problems, and perspective of someone else unless we're willing to listen.

21

In Plain sight

Have you ever spent more time than you want to admit looking for something–and then realize it had been lying right in front of you all the time? The more you struggle to find solutions to problems (or answers to prayers), the less apt you are to recognize them. Take a break from looking. And then look again!

22 *Be a Smart Investor*

Invest wisely. Your money, of course, but also your abilities, energy, resources, attention, and time. Use what you have to help, strengthen, and benefit others. It might be the moment you take to comfort a child, or listen to a troubled coworker, or check in on an elderly neighbor. Invest yourself–love pays huge dividends.

23 *Back at You!*

The decisions you make and the actions you take–whether major or minor, public or known to only a few–bear your imprint. Integrity, honesty, dedication, commitment, and high principles leave their mark, and it all reflects back on you. Look to God's guidelines, and the things you do are bound to look good on you!

24 *Count the Cost*

If you spend more than your budget allows, trouble is just around the corner. It's true with money, and also with your time and energy. Over-committing yourself exhausts the number of hours you have in a day, and drains your supply of energy, too. Just as you budget your money, budget your time, too. Neither is limitless!

25

There Beside You

A circle of friends who are at your stage in life is your best support group. They can provide real-time advice, understanding, and encouragement as only fellow travelers can give. Together you can compare notes on relationships, health, family, and personal well-being. They have a unique perspective–not because they've been there, but because they are there!

26

Eyes Have It

People hear words, but believe their eyes. Are your observable strengths, talents, and abilities matching the strengths, talents, and abilities you tell them you possess? If there's a gap between what you say about yourself and the behavior that people see, guess what they're going to believe?

27 *Unpack Your Bags*

Life is a journey, but if you're carrying around a suitcase full of old losses and past regrets, you've got excess baggage. There's a hefty charge for that, one you'll pay with years of pining, sadness, and gloom. Get rid of that load! For life's journey, just as for your next trip, the less luggage you carry, the lighter you travel!

28 *Pleased with People*

If being around friends brings on anxiety and discomfort, maybe it's because you're focusing on yourself instead of on them. You don't have to impress them with your smarts or achievements, and, unless you're hosting the event, it's not up to you to be their source of entertainment. Relax, be yourself, and enjoy the people around you!

29 *The Middle Ground*

When it comes to income, right in the middle is the best place to be. If you're not rolling in money, be glad. You're not tempted to measure yourself by how many possessions you can accumulate. If you're not scraping by on a pittance, give thanks. You get to enjoy life's simple delights, and they're always the best ones!

September

30

Learn a Lesson

Make use of the lessons life teaches you by learning from them. Study each life lesson that comes your way long and deeply enough to understand what happened and why it happened. Plan to make better decisions next time. The last thing you want is to be taught life lessons more than once!

October

1

Muffle the Echo

When you only pay attention to opinions you agree with, you're closing yourself in an echo chamber. You hear what supports your views, not what might broaden them. Diversify your listening, reading, and news-watching choices. You might still hold onto your original judgment, but you'll also discover other ways of seeing things.

2

You Choose It

Every day, you have a wide range of choices available to you. Perhaps going to the dentist's office is a must, but how you feel about it is your choice. Eating food is a must, but what (and how much) you put in your mouth is your choice. Your obligations are a must, but the way you go about them is your choice. Today, make the best choices!

3 *Get Yourself Started*

If you're a little bit nervous at the prospect of an upcoming interview, meeting, or class reunion, take some time beforehand to sit quietly and picture yourself in the situation. In your mind, compose positive, relevant, and appropriate comments that you might make. With a few conversation starters tucked away, the rest will come naturally!

4 *Eyes on You*

It's important to pay attention to others, and it's equally important to pay attention to yourself. Explore your thoughts and observations by reflecting on your experiences. Spend quiet time to think things through, or write in a journal, or express yourself through art or poetry. Get–and stay–acquainted with you!

5 *Key to Renewal*

Recall a special situation, event, or experience that left you feeling renewed and rejuvenated. What about it was key to your enjoyment? If it was meeting new people, enroll in a class or join a club that meets in your town. If it was being spa-pampered, make a space in your home your private getaway. If it was learning, discovering, and exploring new things, visit your local library!

6 *Magnificence of You*

Explore the world around you, and not just the one you can see with your eyes. Look beyond majestic sunsets and starry skies and ponder the mystery of creation, its infinite beauty, and the God who made it happen. Look beyond the face you see in the mirror and contemplate the magnificence of your soul and spirit...of you.

7 *Get It Done*

You might have been putting it off for a long time, but if it needs to be done, why not do it today? Procrastination only prolongs the agony. Get it marked off the to-do list so you won't have to keep seeing it pop up week after week. And you might even want to promise yourself a little treat to celebrate the "done" checkmark!

8 *Fire It Up!*

Join a book club, and you're bound to read books and authors far outside your usual choices. Enroll in a music appreciation class, and you'll listen to selections beyond those you've downloaded on your phone. These are just two examples of ways to broaden your knowledge, and perhaps ignite a whole new life passion! What would fire you up?

9 *Look for Good*

If you think most people are rude, you're sure to find a lot of rude people out there! If you believe that most people are friendly and kindhearted, guess what? You'll run into friendly and kindhearted people on a daily basis. It's true–when you go out looking for it, you're sure to find it. For your own happiness, look for good.

10 *A Weak Spot*

Everyone has strengths, but no one is strong in every way. By being honest and objective in facing your weaknesses, you can do something about them. You might discover how to best cope with your weak areas by upping your skills, relying on the strengths of others, or asking for help or advice when you need it.

11 *For Best Results*

Before you act on an impulse to help someone with what you consider a problem, take time to think through possible outcomes. Is the person asking for and open to your involvement? Have you shared your idea with them to see if it's what they would find helpful? Sometimes the best intended action ends in unintended consequences.

12 *A Decorating Tip*

Wherever you live, make a special place for at least one item that you love. It might be a picture, bowl or vase, or piece of furniture that brings a good feeling every time you look at it. If it's functional too, that's fine. But if it warms your heart and makes you smile, that's function enough!

13 *Outlook on Life*

Life is...what? Note the word that popped into your head. If it's negative, cynical, or sarcastic, ask yourself why. Perhaps you've allowed difficult circumstances to overshadow everyday blessings, or the pessimistic views of others are coloring your perspective. If life is less than good, try looking again, but this time with the eyes of your heart. The good in life begins there.

14 *Giving and Receiving*

Some of us are thoughtful and generous givers. We love shopping for just the right gift for our friends and loved ones, and we beam with pleasure when they're delighted with what we've selected. But we're uncomfortable receivers. If this describes you, allow others the pleasure of giving, too, by receiving with genuine joy and heartfelt gratitude.

15 *Away with Worry!*

Worry is more than a waste of time. It's a mood-dampener and energy-sapper. What's more, it's not helping your problem one bit, only loading it up with fearful imaginings and scary scenarios. Replace worry with prayer. God hears, cares, and relieves your worries by comforting you with faith in His power to see you through.

16 *Time Well Spent*

For a few days, list the things you read and watch online and note how long you spend with each. Are you surprised? Is too much of your time frittered away going from video to video, reading lengthy newsfeeds, or clicking on ads? Maybe you'll want to check out some informative discussion groups, positive and inspirational stories and videos, or online education sources. Make your online time, time well spent!

17 *Do-Nothing Day*

Relax. Sleep in. Putter around the house or garden with no particular goal in mind. Page through a magazine and look at the pictures. Stare at the sky and count all the cloud-critters you see. Watch a bumble bee bounce from blossom to blossom in search of nectar. Take time out once in a while for no other purpose than to do nothing!

18 *Here and Now*

Maybe there's a meeting or appointment on your calendar that you're not looking forward to. But it's not happening today, is it? Then refuse to think about it so you can more fully concentrate on–and enjoy–your here and now. The happier and less stressed you are when the time comes for the tough stuff, the easier you're likely to get through it.

19 *Judge for Yourself*

Judging others and judging their behavior are two different things. The first puts you in the role of God, who alone knows whether a person's motivations are "good" or "bad." The second places you as one who can hear words and observe actions only, and comment on those only. Remember the difference whenever you're talking about other people.

20 *A Priceless Gift*

Imagine the burden of holding a grudge against a loved one. Picture the grief of one who would like to make amends, but who finds herself rebuffed at every turn. Rifts between friends and family members bring nothing but sadness for all, a sadness that can span years, decades, even a lifetime. Give yourself, and offer others, the priceless gift of reconciliation.

21 *The Constant Critic*

If you're engaged in the business of life, you're bound to run up against those who tell you that you're doing it all wrong! Listen to what they say, but be able to separate fact from fiction. If you're not sure whether their criticism has validity, check it out with a trusted friend or counselor. Act on what's useful, and send the rest away in the wind.

22 *Are You Kidding?*

Have you ever been kidded about something? Trouble is, it hit home–maybe a feature or characteristic you're self-conscious about, or something you did once that you don't want to be reminded of for the rest of your life. You grin and bear it, but it hurts inside. So speak gently. What's meant as good-natured kidding can come across as anything but.

23

A Good Encounter

Sitting at an outdoor café or on a park bench, you might enjoy people-watching. No doubt you see a few interesting fashion statements, and maybe glean a couple tantalizing tidbits of conversation. But how much more rewarding it would be to actually talk to the lone coffee-drinker at the next table, or chat with the woman pushing a stroller! Next time, make it a one-on-one for your sake–and for theirs.

24

No More Fears!

Fears keep you captive. The more fears, the smaller the cage. Break loose by naming and tackling your fears one by one. Do you fear future loneliness, ill-health, financial hardship, job loss? Address each fear with practical steps you can take to avoid what you fear. And don't forget to ask God for the strength to overcome any difficulties you may actually face now or in the future.

25

It's Your Choice

No one can make you happy. Not that they don't want to, but they don't have the power to do it! At the same time, you can't make anyone else happy, because if they haven't already chosen happiness, there's no way you can give it to them. A happy frame of mind comes from the inside, and you're responsible for choosing yours, just as everyone else is responsible for choosing theirs.

26 *A Caring Response*

Before you take offense at someone's attitude toward you, take into account what that person might be going through. Their home situation, health concerns, job worries, financial crisis, and spiritual struggles have nothing to do with you, but happened to spill out in a brusque remark or unkind turn. Instead of adding to the person's burden, lighten it with a smile that says, "I understand."

27 *A Scorekeeper's Job*

In competitive games, scorekeepers are responsible for tracking each team's points and plays. The game of life, however, needs no self-appointed scorekeepers. By insisting on tit-for-tat, deciding who owes what to whom, and rating others against their own expectations, scorekeepers create disharmony and weaken morale. Leave scorekeeping to the pros at the sports complex–that's their job! You? That's not what you do.

28 *Note to Self*

Ask an elderly person what they most regret, and you probably won't hear about not making more money, having a bigger house, or working longer hours. Likely laments? Failing to forgive... holding onto resentments...accepting disrespect or mistreatment for so long...not believing in themselves...neglecting their real needs. Is there something you're doing today that you might regret later in life?

29 *The Light Side*

Treat yourself lightly! Not every social stumble calls for a massive apology and the throes of self-mortification. Your awkward moment is not going to stay forever at the center of everyone's thoughts. One mistake doesn't mean you're the most incompetent person who's ever walked on Earth. A simple acknowledgement and a little humor will do–and then move on!

30 *The Dream Gap*

A lot of people have big dreams, but few actually make them happen. Most often it's because the gap between a big dream and big achievement is filled with hard work. That means channeling your time, attention, and effort to making your dream come true. Sacrificing today's pleasure for tomorrow's success. Using setbacks as stepping stones to going forward. Are you willing to close the gap?

October

31 *List So Far*

Instead of listing adventures you'd like to experience and the places you'd like to go, try adding up all the adventures you've already had and the places you've already been. When you're done, you might be surprised to realize that so far the journey from where you started has been nothing short of amazing!

November

1 *Comparisons and Contracts*

You are you, with your own combination of talents, skills, interests, and objectives. The person you envy for one thing might lack something you possess in abundance. All the time you waste wishing you had a trait you don't have leaves less time for appreciating and enhancing the traits you do have. Contrasts between people are obvious facts, but comparisons are heartbreaking self-judgments.

2 *Keep the Bridge*

Even if you'd like to change it sooner or later, you are where you are right now. Make the most of it by noting the good and learning from the challenges. If you're looking to change, make an exit plan that attests to your integrity and character. Leave as many good feelings and intact relationships as you can. It doesn't pay to burn bridges, because you never know when you might need to cross them!

3 *Learn the Basics*

An objective record of solid achievement is a far better foundation for succeeding at complex, higher-level projects than an inflated description of dazzling accomplishments. Of course this applies to the workplace, but also to everyday life. Gourmet cooking? Expert beekeeper? Noted artist? Published poet? Master the basics. Real success comes when it's built on a foundation of facts.

4 *Your Good Word*

When you say you're going to do something, do you follow through? If there's a string of broken promises behind you, look for a recurring pattern. Perhaps you habitually overpromise...allow any blip in your plans to deter you from keeping your promise...excuse yourself if you just don't feel like doing it. What needs to happen so others can depend on you to keep your word?

5 *A Nighttime Prayer*

When you turn the light out at night, give the day a gentle good-bye. Thank the day for the blessings it brought you, accept the challenges it has brought to you, and treasure in your heart the joyful memories it made possible. Then sleep in peaceful expectation that tomorrow will come with more blessings, more memories, and increased ability to handle whatever comes your way.

6 *It's a Plan*

No matter how tight your budget is right now, don't deprive yourself of the privilege of giving. A small percentage of your income donated to assist those who live on less than you allows you to express compassion and generosity. A few cans to the food pantry every week does it, too. Planned, consistent giving to others puts your trust in God to see you through your own difficulties.

7 *It's Only Natural*

You can't help but notice how, when you start out the day by doing or saying something nice to someone, the whole day seems to go better for you. There's nothing magic about it! Your early-on good turn made you feel good about yourself, and when you feel good about yourself, it's only natural you'll feel good about everyone else!

8 *Little Bits Count*

Little choices you make from day to day can make big changes. Say you choose to set your alarm fifteen minutes early every day to give yourself a calmer, saner, more doable morning. No big deal each day, but quite a bit when it becomes so much a part of your routine that you can't believe you ever went without it. Now that counts!

9 *Thoughts Gone Wild*

Oh, those things that ping into your brain and seem so funny at the time! But not all of them are what you want remembered, much less repeated or posted, by those around you. Those words will rarely make you look as witty as you felt at the moment. Reign in your thoughts and sift them through a fine-screened filter before they get out of your mouth!

10 *Feelings Follow Actions*

So you're feeling grumpy today. Well, join the human race! From time to time, everyone wakes up feeling out-of-sorts. But it doesn't have to be a bad day for you, or for those around you. Acknowledge your mood, but decide that your feelings aren't going to have the final say. Stand up straight, put on a friendly face, and tell that grumpy mood good-bye!

11 *Words of Wisdom*

You're urged to spend, save, and invest wisely. You might think it's just about money, but it's also about time. Though wealth differs among people, time does not. It's the same 24/7 for all of us. So what are you doing with yours? Are you spending it on activities that matter, using "saved time" rather than frittering it away, and investing it in worthwhile pursuits? Only you've got it!

12 *Around the Block*

A lot of people know things, but not everyone is willing to share what they know. Like a miser with money, they keep their knowledge close to the chest, only to be brought out when they can parade it among others. You've been around the block a time or two! Be a generous sharer with those who could–and will–be blessed by your knowledge and experience.

13 *As Wind Blows*

If you don't like what's happening, what can you do to change it? You're not a buoy bobbing in the sea, tilting this direction or that, depending on the wind. Okay, you can't change which way the wind blows, but you do have the ability to tilt in a different direction. Do one thing that will give you a feeling of control!

14 *Bigger and Better*

Describe your fondest, most secret dream. Now play the cool-eyed examiner–you. Is this dream worth today's continued care and attention? If yes, then how can you feasibly and practically pursue it? If no, give it a big hug, a pat on the head, and let it loose. You've outgrown it, and you realize that there are bigger, better things out there worth dreaming about!

15 *Share the Blessings*

If you have had enough to eat today and a roof over your head, you have more than many alive in the world. No, it's impossible to banish hunger and homelessness from the face of the Earth all by yourself, but one full bag of groceries to a food pantry, or one hour's work at a shelter each week can ease one person's scarcity–and add to your abundance.

16 *Time Will Tell*

Make responsible plans for your future, but at the same time remain flexible today. Accept the setbacks and game-changers that come along, because they are part of life. Similarly, don't close yourself off to unforeseen opportunities that come your way, because they could open a whole new world to you. Make plans that include God's good will for you!

17 *Enjoying the Peace*

When things get chaotic, the excitement spreads. Every day brings a surprising development to talk about, fresh news to post, share, and speculate on. How dull it seems when peace breaks out again! Don't let chaos be the norm. Embrace peace to the fullest. Take deep breaths. Stretch. Enjoy. Avoid the temptation to crave another bombshell!

18 *It Comes Around*

When the people around you are relaxed and happy, you're relaxed and happy, too, right? That's why making your world a safe place for others works in your favor. Doing everything you can to make those around you comfortable also assures your comfort. When consideration, thoughtfulness, respect, and tolerance goes around, it comes around!

19 *A Simple Smile*

It takes courage and self-confidence to go around smiling, you know! Some people might wonder what mischief you've been up to, but most will smile back. They'll get a grin-lift for sure, and maybe a few might have a few friendly words for you. Does that sound so bad? It must, because not many of us are brave enough to risk a simple smile!

20 *Use His Gifts*

Everything you own and all the blessings you have received are God's gifts to you. Appreciate the possessions and opportunities He gives you, but don't hoard them like a miser with a bag of coins! Use each gift as God intends for your well-being, comfort, and pleasure, and for the well-being, comfort, and pleasure of others.

21 *Sieze the Day!*

There never will be another time like the present! The unique combination of people and events around you, as well as your perception, feelings, and response never will come together in quite the same way that they are right now. Pick up on the nuances and subtle meanings the day brings. Use each moment to learn more about life, living, and you!

22 *World of Difference*

You might not be on the world stage (or want to be), but that doesn't excuse you from actively participating in life and among people. Engage yourself in pursuits and causes you care about, because the positive difference you and others make locally can make a positive difference globally. When you work for the better, the world can't help but get better, too!

23 *Expect an Answer*

When you pray for something, expect a response. An answer is something God promises to give you! So keep your eyes open for the blessing you requested...or for another blessing your wise God knows will work much better for you...or for a gentle heart-hug and a whisper to wait a little, because the time just isn't quite right yet. Pray, and then watch!

24 *Just a Pinch*

Add a pinch of dirt to a glass of pure water, it isn't pure water anymore. You'll probably take a pass on drinking it! Similarly, truth is truth. Once it's bent or stretched, embellished or embroidered, detracted from or added to, it's no longer the truth. When you speak, don't ask others to swallow a lie. In the future, they will take what you say with, well, a pinch of dirt.

25 *Invite a Friend*

When you face a challenge, use your abilities to the fullest. Think through your options, plan your best course of action, and then put all your effort toward realizing a good outcome. But most important, pray. Lay it all out in front of Him, because He has the ability to see you through!

26 *Act of Courage*

Courage, like any other character trait, can be used wisely–or not. Handled foolishly, courage leads to reckless gambles, thoughtless risks, and the pursuit of ill-advised goals and objectives. Managed wisely, however, your courage gives you the confidence you to go out on a limb when you need to and take calculated risks that open you to a fuller, richer, and more satisfying future.

27 *It Saves Lives*

We bristle when we're told "no." But sometimes it's what we need to hear from God, from those who care about us, and from ourselves. If we're contemplating an ill-advised move, asking for something that would put us in harm's way, or starting to adopt unhealthy habits, "no" isn't only our best friend–it's our lifesaver.

28 *Have a System*

The busier you are, the more organization pays off. With all your to-do's and appointments written down, you don't have to keep prodding yourself to remember them all. With a specific drop-point for your car keys, you never need to run around looking for them. Make getting–and staying–organized a priority. Spend your time doing the things you want to do, not hunting for your cellphone!

29 *The Anonymous Angel*

Make life a little easier for someone just for the joy of it. Maybe it's the criticism you keep to yourself, the good word you put in for them, or the silent prayer you say for them. Perhaps you're the "anonymous" who does that little favor that kept them smiling for a week! Not every kindness needs the limelight.

30 *Sweets for You*

A treat doesn't always have to consist of chocolate! Maybe you'd actually prefer something else, like a quiet stroll outside, a leisurely manicure and pedicure, an hour window shopping with a friend, an afternoon puttering in the garden. And if you choose to top it off with a bite of chocolate, all the sweeter!

DECEMBER

1 *All for Love*

Doing what you love today might not be feasible or practical, but you can love what you do. Banish auto-pilot and pay attention to the things you see, the voices you hear, and the textures you touch. Be aware of various scents. Immerse yourself in what you're doing at the moment rather than going by rote. You might find that you're doing a lot of things you love after all!

2 *A Happy Idea*

When you receive a complimentary or congratulatory email, save it to a folder marked "My Happiness File." Whenever you need a mood-booster or a reminder of how much you're loved and cared about, click open the folder. One by one, look through the emails. Say the name of each sender, and as you finish reading their message, ask God to send a happy blessing to them.

3 *Color Your Life*

If you like to relax with a set of colored pencils and a book of designs, you know that the colors you choose determine the overall mood and appeal of the finished picture. The colors you choose for your home, your clothes, and your make-up work the same way. "Color" your surroundings and yourself with hues that bring out the best in you!

4 *Take a Stretch*

Everyone who takes exercising seriously occasionally stretches a muscle too far. It's painful, but the worst thing you can do is stop exercising! Sure, go easy on it for a day or so, but keep moving. Do the same when you stretch your abilities but fail to reach your goal. Pull back, reposition, but don't stop stretching yourself. One day you'll be in perfect shape to make it!

5 *A Healthy Diet*

Flattering words sound sweet, but as they go in one ear, quickly chase them out the other. Savored flattery puts you under the control of the person feeding it to you, and swallowed flattery fattens the ego, weighing it down with delusions of self-importance. Accept and appreciate earned praise, but walk away from flattery and those who attempt to whet your appetite for it.

6

Get a Clue

Your friends and loved ones may hesitate to burden you with their problems, but you can usually pick up visual and verbal clues that something just isn't right. Give them your full attention, express your concern, and then allow them to open up to you and share what is on their heart.

7

A Whole Heart

Tough times come into everyone's life. Many even endure losses of epic proportions and injustices that carry lifetime consequences. Though some sufferers will give in to bitterness, others manage to rise above it. By strength of will, commitment to high principles, and firm reliance on God's power to bring healing, you can be among those who survive with a loving heart intact.

8 *Confront Conflict Now*

A conflict between you and a friend or loved one might seem so insignificant that you decide not to bring it up again. After all, who wants to appear small or petty? But if you keep thinking about it, resentment will soon play a very big, very significant, role in your relationship. Confront small conflicts before they have a chance to grow into major quarrels.

9 *First Aid Kit*

Compile a folder (paper or cyber, it doesn't matter) of spiritual thoughts, upbeat quotes, positive messages, heartwarming stories, pictures that make you smile, and jokes that make you laugh. Open it when you're feeling gloomy or when life just loses its luster. It's your first aid kit for heart and soul!

10 *Look at Me!*

So you're debuting a sexy new look. The first time you go out, you're convinced that everyone you meet is staring at you in complete disapproval! It's highly unlikely, but even if you should notice a raised eyebrow, so what? You're not dressing for a passing stranger, but for yourself–and perhaps also for the appreciation and complete approval of someone you love!

11 *Say and Do*

A lot of words with no action to support them are meaningless. That goes particularly for words of love. The most eloquent expressions of love fall flat unless they're backed up with loving actions. Repeated protestations of love ring hollow unless substantiated by consistent kindness, tenderness, and respect. Never settle for only words.

12 *Into the Trash!*

Scammers and phishers hope your curiosity will get the best of you. So you're offered a free cruise? You've won a contest you didn't enter? You're chosen (out of everyone in the world!) to help a stranger deposit a check? Resist the urge to see what it's all about. Once you've clicked, you've taken the bait, and you haven't won, but they have!

13 *Save the Scene*

Not every problem you encounter warrants a dramatic scene. Before your emotions take over, examine the issue and see exactly what happened and what's at stake. Determine if you're the best one to handle it, and if so, what you plan to do about it. You might have it solved before the diva in you gets a chance to step on stage!

14 *New and Improved*

Sometimes a new season in life or change in circumstance calls for a make-over. A milestone birthday might get you thinking about a more up-to-date look. A workplace promotion might prompt you to up your social skills. Positive change, however, never goes against your principles or values, or presents you as someone you're not. The enhanced, improved you is still you!

15

Busy Being Busy?

There's keeping busy...and doing busy work. When you're actively engaged in productive activity, you're using your skills and advancing your knowledge and abilities. At day's end, you're tired, but it's a good kind of tired. The day has been exhilarating and purposeful. Doing busy work, however, leaves you exhausted with nothing to show for it. If this is you, get busy finding something worth your time and talents!

16

Way To Go!

If you can't see which way to turn, try this. Describe to God your specific circumstances as you understand them, as objectively as possible. When you're finished, don't go into why you believe this direction or that won't work, or why you can't get there from here. Just sit still and listen! Let Him read the map and show you His way to go.

17

You've Earned It

"The world doesn't owe you anything." Does the statement bring a frown or a smile? You might frown if you expect reward without effort, gain without pain. But if you smile, you've discovered the joy of earned success and you thrive on meeting goals and surpassing expectations. The world might not owe you anything, but it has plenty to give you–and it will!

18

Share the Joy

When you come across a story that makes you laugh out loud, an image that leaves you in awe, or an idea that just might work, share it! Let others in on the humor and double your own. Talk about what inspires you–it could be exactly what will inspire someone else. Invite others to see another point of view, because it could change their world!

19

Make It Real

If the posts of your faraway friends leave you feeling that they're having all the fun, turn off your device and call a near-to-you friend. Plan an afternoon or evening out, or better yet, a day trip to someplace neither of you have visited. Chances are good that she's ready for some face-to-face time and a real-time adventure!

20

Practice Preventative Medicine

Physical symptoms tell you it's time to visit your physician, and ongoing stress signals that it's time for a break. You might be able to carry on as usual, hiding the true state of your emotions from others, but the tension is still there. Before you hit the crisis point, take time out. It's not just for your peace of mind, but for the health of it.

21 *Get It Done!*

If there's a tedious, difficult, or unpleasant task you need to do, put it first on your to-do list. Ideally, tackle it first thing in the morning when you're fresh and have the most energy. Get it done, cross it off the list, and enjoy the rest of your day!

22 *Learn New Tricks*

No matter where you are in life, don't settle for what you already know and what you're able to do. It's never too late (or too early) to adopt the habit of lifelong learning. Explore, discover, and keep those "aha!" moments coming! You need them–they'll perk up your life, and your brain and creativity, too!

23 *Trust Your Gut*

When those who have made it big talk about their way up, they'll usually mention a time when they almost gave up the struggle. Opportunities weren't coming, doors weren't opening. Friends and family members urged them to quit. But they had a gut feeling that they could make it–and they did. When your intuition and others' advice differ, trust your gut.

24 *Wherever You Are*

God is everywhere, you know. There's no need to wait until later to give Him a word of praise or thanks, or go to another place to ask Him for His help. If it's on your mind right now, talk to God about it right now where you are.

25 *Strategy and Spontaneity*

Have a strategy. Know where you're headed and how you plan to get there. But, at the same time, remain open to spontaneous experience. Take a break for the sake of renewal and refreshment, and mostly for the sheer joy of it. Faithfully followed strategy and freedom-loving spontaneity are a winning combination!

26

Keep in Touch

Keep in touch with friends and family members in a way that makes it easy for them to keep in touch with you. While some may welcome a phone call, others may respond more readily to letters, emails, texts, or posts on social networking sites. Your willingness to discover and follow their preference is a gift from you to them every time they hear from you!

27

Never Accept Invisibility!

Your existence is proof that God means for you to be seen and heard. If you've been feeling invisible lately, give yourself a maintenance check. Are you standing in the shadows and walking with slumping shoulders and downcast eyes? Are you wearing drab, don't-look-at-me clothing? Are you speaking in tentative whispers? A few visible (and audible) tweaks should do the trick!

28

Exercise for Fun

If your exercise plan doesn't float your boat, abandon ship. Try something else–like swimming, for instance, or team sports, or dancing, or inline skating. Exercise that you enjoy doing not only revitalizes your body, but energizes your mind and spirit, too. For smooth sailing to better health and a sunny mood, exercise for fun!

29 *A World Transformed*

Say there's something about your life that you'd like to change. But you see only two choices: you force a change that negatively impacts others, or you let things go on as they are. Often there's a third choice. Slowly implement small changes that may make things better for you. Gently and consistently insist on personal boundaries. Work less toward rapid change than toward positive transformation.

30 *Use Your Head!*

If you work with numbers all day, give your brain a break with a daily crossword puzzle or word game. But if you work with words, challenge yourself with Sudoku. So you're talking to people all day or running from one appointment to the next? Relax with something that requires mind-centering concentration, like a logic puzzle or find-the-differences picture. Let your brain in on the games!

31 *Be a Peacemaker*

Even among good friends, conversations can get heated. When you realize that the temperature's rising, don't sweat. Kindly, lighthearted humor is like a cooling breeze, dispelling some of the hot air and giving everyone a chance to take a deep breath and shift to a more appropriate topic. Be the one who knows how to turn down the thermostat!